PRAIS

"In this Age of AI, every function in every company has to go through its own digital transformation to enable their organizations to succeed. Glenn Hopper provides an essential roadmap to accounting and finance executives on how to embrace analytics and AI as core tools for modern finance. This book should be a required reading for every general manager."
Karim R. Lakhani | Dorothy and Michael Hintze Professor of Business Administration, Co-Director of Laboratory for Innovation Science at Harvard, and Co-Chair of Harvard Business Analytics Program

"Glenn vouches for innovation and upgrades in a straightforward way that shows his experience in the field and the success of embracing finance automation. There's no way around it - you need to know this material in order to stay ahead of the pack!"
Orad Elkayam | Founder, Mogi Group

"The big ideas of democratizing data and undergoing a digital transformation, Glenn points out, are common sense in the Information Age. All CFOs should pick up a copy!"
Rick Yvanovich, FCMA, CGMA, FCPA, MSC, CCMP, CMC | CEO, TRG

"At a time when everyone is talking about digital transformations, automation, and the promise of artificial intelligence, Deep Finance serves as a commonsense guide for finance professionals hoping to transform corporate finance into a streamlined business unit that not only provides efficient and accurate financial information, but also leads the charge for a company's transition to a data-driven organization."
Eric Friedrichsen | CEO, Board Director at Emburse

"Easy to read, but still insightful -- Deep Finance is a launching pad for discussions among your finance team and the leaders in the C-suite. If your company is trying to move into the next era of accounting, you've got to read this book."
**Renee Becker Bourbeau | Director of Operations
& Master of Science in Business Analytics (MSBA),
Graduate Career Management Center (GCMC),
Goizueta Business School | Emory University**

"Deep Finance shows how business intelligence and analytics are fundamentally tied to the finance function. In this book, Glenn Hopper illustrates a path for leaders in corporate finance & accounting departments to use these skills along with automation and data science to transform their organizations from within. Through increased automation and more intelligent use of information,

financial leaders can propel their organizations into a new era."
Michael Whitmire | CEO and Co-founder of FloQast

"Financial transformation is both the greatest challenge and greatest opportunity for CFOs and their teams. But the path forward remains uncertain. In Deep Finance, Glenn Hopper outlines a pragmatic approach that can be implemented by finance leaders to transform financial operations in a way that will create a long-term competitive advantage for the companies they lead."
Jack McCullough | President & Founder, CFO Leadership Council, Author, *Secrets of Rockstar CFOs*

"The future of effective, game changing analytics belongs to finance. Glenn captures the essence of why. As a core pillar of any organization, CFO's and finance teams are in a prime position to help leverage and champion the strategic, organizational, and cultural transformation that is needed to succeed with data and analytics. Glenn's book highlights how finance professionals can use data and analytics as a strategic force multiplier for their business."
Jason Krantz | CEO/Founder, Strategy Titan

"Glenn hits the nail on the head over and over again regarding the democratization of data and how to find the hidden messages buried in the enormous amounts of data organizations can capture. If you have heard the acronyms "RPA", "ML", and "AI", but are unsure of what they are or what they mean for managing a modern, digitally enabled business, Glenn lays it all out in a consumable and usable approach to a highly complex topic."

Dave Weiss | Director, Advisory Services, NetSuite and Salesforce Practice, Spaulding Ridge, LLC

"Glenn's vision to transform today's CFO into 'The New Age CFO' is not only brilliant but financially prudent, and practical to implement. A must read for all companies eager to strategically and successfully compete in today's digital economy."

**Cynthia A. Conway | CEO Chair,
Vistage Worldwide, Inc.**

"From Fortune 500 companies all the way down to brand new startups, the automation steps laid out in Deep Finance are crucial for companies looking to transition to the next phase of financial reporting. This would be an amazing reference for establishing a finance department for a new company. Imagine having everything in place right from the beginning. That's where I'd love to see this outline applied."

Aaron Vick | Author of *Leaderpreneur: A Leadership Guide for Startups and Entrepreneurs & Inevitable Revolutions: Secrets and Strategies for a Successful Business*

"Deep Finance is an invaluable resource for finance pros guiding their company through digital transformation. Even if before reading this book you find yourself asking, 'What is AI?' you'll find the answer in this highly informative, accessible read."
Seth Zimmerman | Senior Vice President, Real Estate at Silverpeak

Leaders Press

ISBN 978-1-63735-124-6 (pbk)
ISBN 978-1-63735-026-3 (e-book)

Library of Congress Control Number:
2020925511

DEEP FINANCE

Corporate Finance in the Information Age

GLENN HOPPER

Leaders
Press

Table of Contents

FOREWORD

by Scott Culbertson

I believe there are only a few people in any crowd that are wired to think up new ideas. Just a handful among any population. But we only need a few visionaries around us to point us in these new directions. It will be up to everyone else to see it, travel it, and help bring the new vision to reality. Once a new pathway has been paved for all to see, adoption sets in. Others can begin to visualize the pathway for themselves, observe its color, its width, its challenges, and its possibilities and perhaps see themselves walking down that path—or perhaps launching into a full sprint, as I so often like to do.

The pages in this book set you on a journey to discover the realm of a new possibility addressed to all types of business professionals and those interested in becoming business leaders. Here, those of you serving in a finance capacity will begin to see new pathways and new possibilities that were unseen before. Business leaders, you will see a new realm of possibility that will change your behavior and impact your bottom line. In my opinion, the information shared should be embraced by all businesses, large and small.

I grew up as a young CPA, bouncing from business to business doing what I loved—managing financial data, building financial statements, interpreting financials based on the numbers on the page, and managing great people that helped me live my passion. You might say that I was involved in the business, but I really wasn't. This was important work, but I was hidden in the corner, doing my job, pushing financial figures around spreadsheets and financial statements. Along with the financial information I had at my disposal, there were always business data, metrics, and other non-financial numbers that were nearby—headcounts, product units, product rates— that helped us evaluate the trends on the financial statements from month to month. We would write up our commentary and hope that the business understood what we had to say.

Over time, I found myself leaving the financial statements to other people while I dove deeper into the business. I dove so deep I found myself running a sales team, then running operational teams, then building new teams for functions that hadn't existed before, developing new products, and now, influencing all areas of a company. Through all these stages in my career, my finance and CPA experience never departed. That hat was never put on the shelf. I needed it to succeed as my career transformed over time.

New pathways exist when you deeply integrate the finance function into the organization. The last three companies I worked for, I was successful because I partnered with finance. There is no easier way to put it. I knew I needed them. I knew they had information I wanted. And I knew I had a wealth of information that they needed. Together, we moved the business.

I recently had the pleasure of meeting Glenn Hopper through a new business venture that brought us together. After a few conversations, it was clear that he has the success formula for the world I was living. This book is that code, a refreshing paradigm shift in how the finance function should be engaged and deeply embedded within the business. Our conversations were rather surreal, even magical. Glenn reveals the structure so that you and I can take advantage of what a big data business world has to offer—for our careers, our teams, and for the benefits of our investors, and most importantly, our clients.

Glenn and I are off on our next adventure, building and deploying a global business intelligence platform for an entire industry. We are working to integrate critical platforms and harness data that allows us to identify critical anomalies and predict the future. Our audience is not just CFOs; it includes accountants, project managers, product managers, lawyers, sales leaders, strategists, innovators, our vendors, and even our clients.

What is most exciting is that there is no need to create a new technology to be successful. The technologies are here. And the data is here. We just need people, like you, to bring it together—to map out a new pathway for your organization that will influence healthy behaviors and economics, as well as to do wonderful things for your clients.

This book will present to you a new pathway. Pick up ingredients along the way to help make a difference for your organization and your career. Expect transformation. Expect breakthroughs. And, most importantly, enjoy the journey.

Scott Culbertson
SVP Strategy
Sandline Global

Introduction

Business leaders don't typically associate corporate finance with cutting-edge technology. The basics of accounting, after all, haven't changed much since the introduction of double-entry bookkeeping more than half a millennium ago. Despite the ubiquitous bandying about of the catchy "FinTech" portmanteau, many would be hard pressed to identify major changes in finance beyond cryptocurrencies and the flashy algorithms that drive decisions of many traders and portfolio managers. Corporate finance is typically viewed as slowly and steadily making journal entries and approving expense reports in the background.

As someone who's worked in corporate finance for more than two decades, I can understand how many of us have earned the reputation of being Luddites. I've been in the industry long enough to remember that my first purchasing manager tracked all invoices and purchase orders in a paper ledger. Granted, even at that time in the early 2000s, paper ledgers seemed a bit anachronistic.

As I look back at that era, I realize I entered the profession on the cusp of a massive sea change in the way the work of accounting was done. I saw the last remnants of a fading era that were replaced by a more efficient and accurate system, one driven by technology. And it was that damned paper ledger that set me off on what has become my mission: to propel corporate finance organizations into the new millennium.

A digital transformation might look different depending on the size of your business and the software that your team has already integrated into your everyday processes. In general, it may include

- democratizing the data available to finance departments and departments across the company
- identifying the best Robotic Process Automation (RPA) to automate manual processes
- building or buying an Enterprise Resource Planning (ERP) system and integrating it with current software
- creating a business intelligence team to apply Machine Learning (ML) to data for better analysis

Do not let unfamiliar terms distract you from the end goal. You cannot let your finance department (and overall company) fall behind the way those old paper ledgers and adding machines did in the last transformation. Throughout this book, you will learn the many opportunities that a digital transformation can bring to your business. At best, you will be an innovator in your industry, offering fast turnarounds and better predictions than any competitor who is still using manual processes. At the very least, automating processes and embracing innovative technologies can help you avoid a million dollar mistake.

DON'T LET YOUR FINANCE DEPARTMENT MAKE A MILLION DOLLAR MISTAKE

Early in my finance career, my planned path for advancement was to outwork and outhustle everyone else. I figured that the more responsibilities I could pull into my purview, the more valuable I would be to the company. As an ambitious twenty-something corporate guy with a freshly minted MBA, I worked 70+ hour weeks, constantly looking for ways to expand my corporate domain. And this approach worked—until it didn't.

I managed to grow my dominion enough that I was given my first employee. I didn't get to pick the employee but was glad to have the help. I had grown my responsibilities of tracking spend for a single department to an entire division. My first employee was "Gary," a lifelong purchasing clerk, who had probably forgotten more about procurement and logistics than I would ever learn. Gary was a fountain of knowledge and a stickler for the rules. He was the perfect person to run procurement. He was so good at his job that we all overlooked the fact that he sat at his desk with a big computer he seldom turned on. Gary tracked everything in paper ledgers. He had a meticulous system for recording purchase orders, payments, inventory levels, deliveries, and returns.

His desk was cluttered with mountains of papers that he manipulated with savant-level expertise. He could pull any invoice or requested document from the tangled stacks in seconds. I was young and inexperienced. Who was I to tell this purchasing legend how to use Microsoft Excel or Lotus Notes?

Gary and I worked for a startup technology company that had an annual capital budget of about twenty million dollars. Our typical purchase orders ranged in value from maybe fifty thousand on the low end up to maybe two million on the high side. And Gary tracked all of this. He would give me weekly reports that were sometimes handwritten and sometimes typed in a Word document or an email. I would take these reports and manually enter them into spreadsheets that we used for tracking purposes. The process was cumbersome, but we made it work—until one year, as we were finalizing our annual spend, looking at next year's budget, and preparing for what was likely to be a contentious board meeting, a call from our equipment provider was confusing us. We had an outstanding invoice with them for around one and a half million dollars. Gary and I poured through his ledgers. There was no outstanding purchase order.

They referenced an invoice number of something like 132495 with a date of June 24 for the amount of $1,468,293.02.

"Well, here's the problem!" Gary said. "They've got the wrong invoice. See, this invoice here that we paid is 132496. Dated June 24 in the amount of $1,572,088.08. They've double-billed us!"

We were pretty excited to learn that it was a vendor issue and were really thankful to Gary for taking such detailed notes so we could point out their mistake.

Only it wasn't their mistake. It was ours. Gary had received both invoices at the same time (probably via postal mail) and had thought they were duplicate invoices. The second invoice had never been entered. We had gone months without realizing this, and now we were going to have to head into a board meeting and explain how we'd missed our capital budget by 7.5 percent when we'd been telling them all year we were on pace.

Needless to say, the board meeting was quite painful, and for a while I thought the whole fiasco would lead to the end of my career. But instead it set me on the mission that would become my life's work.

If necessity is the mother of invention, catastrophe is the catalyst that fuels it. After we took our licks from the board of directors, we shifted our focus to ensuring no mistake like this could ever happen in our department again. The paper ledgers were out and unfortunately Gary wasn't far behind. We didn't make Gary the scapegoat of our story. Gary was not terminated for his bookkeeping error. He chose to leave because he did not want to learn a new system. He did not want to let go of the processes he'd used for his entire career. He was not ready to move into the new era of accounting.

Over the next months and years, I was able to build out a fully connected, automated system of inventory and purchasing tracking that gave us near real-time access to information. Once I had more access to data and started automating processes, I was able to grow my team from being a lone contributor and director to a robust team of developers and report writers and Structured Query Language (SQL) experts. With the right tools in place, the sky became the limit for this business intelligence team. By spending less time on manual processes, we could provide insight that wasn't accessible before. The results were phenomenal, both on and off the page. We identified trends, understood customers, and made better predictions that brought us to our goals much faster. Everyone felt like they were doing more than just crunching numbers. The finance department became the de facto source of information for the company when we had barely been given access to that information before.

I didn't stop there. My company had undergone a "digital transformation" of sorts. Forward-thinking companies saw this digital transformation and wanted a similar elevation in their own finance department. So I repeated the same path, learning more about the opportunities available through artificial intelligence (AI), machine learning (ML), and other types of software that were being built and perfected every day. In my current role, I continue to encourage finance teams and whole companies to take a similar path (without making their own million dollar mistakes). We democratize data, automate manual processes, and create systems that eliminate tedious tasks and elevate everyone's role in the company. Smarter predictions are made with more data, time is better spent, and the bottom line increases significantly. The goal of *Deep Finance* is to help you create the same results.

WHO IS THIS BOOK FOR?

Don't let the mention of AI or ML confuse you—this is a book for Chief Financial Officers (CFOs) and anyone looking to bring automation to their finance department. Many CFOs will raise their eyebrows at taking on data-related tasks, but this book is not about how to become a software developer. You do not have to be able to build an app to lead a digital transformation, although you will need to become more familiar with code and software development. Do not worry about that yet.

This book introduces the basics of technology in accounting, starting with the printing press. As accountants have encountered new forms of technology (punch cards, Excel, Quickbooks, etc.), they have had to make a choice. Do they step into a new age and use these new tools, or get left behind?

Today, the finance world must make a similar choice. Do they step into a new age of AI, ML, and big data, or will they stay in the shadows? For many, the choice to step forward feels like exposing themselves and the members of their field to an inevitable replacement by robots, but this isn't correct. I will explain why as I run through the basics of AI, ML, data science, and RPA. These concepts may have already influenced your processes at work—they are a part of every smart technology in our homes, cars, and offices. They aren't going to replace accountants; they will actually give them better, more fulfilling jobs. By understanding the basics of what these technologies can do, we can see the opportunities available within finance automation and beyond.

In order to seize these opportunities, you and your team (whether you have one already or need to build one) must make a plan. This requires thinking like a coder and speaking the language of developers and data experts. If you haven't partnered with these players yet, you will learn how to bring them onto your team and manage them properly in later chapters. Along the way, you will transform yourself into the New Age CFO, the leader that your company needs in this new age of analytics.

Ultimately, this book is about riding the wave that has always pushed a finance department's role forward in business. Without the right tools, you and your team might feel like a bunch of bean counters who don't add significant value to your company. Many finance departments feel this way, and they are at the highest risk of being left behind as the wave brings more forward-thinking competitors into the age of analytics. *Deep Finance* will help you ride the wave with your competitors, shed the burden of manual processes, and spend your time on higher-level tasks. Its effects are empowering, and, although it will take work, you will start to see the payoff immediately.

For now, let's go back to the beginning. The history of accounting has been shaped by innovations in technology, and the transformations that finance departments are making today are no different.

PART 1.

The History (and Future) of Accounting

I.

We don't just celebrate technological developments for the sake of achievement. We see, with each new advancement in technology, the potential to take a step closer to a fully automated world. Technology has transformed the business landscape in industries ranging from agriculture to zoology. Accounting and finance functions are no exception. A quick look at the history and future of technology in accounting shows how much the profession has changed since the introduction of modern machines.

When I first made the connection between AI, ML, and accounting, I was truly excited to see the potential of how the field and the daily lives of analysts could change dramatically. I started to see and understand how a digital transformation could elevate and empower us to cut through the noise to find meaning and wisdom behind the numbers and add even greater value to our organizations.

Before we look at the potential future of accounting, it is important, I think, to take a step back and look at where we've been.

It's incredible to consider how far technology has advanced in such a short period of human history. The printing press, for example, was developed by Johannes Gutenberg in 1440 and first used commercially in 1450. Now, less than six hundred years later, AI-driven computer software can write text nearly indistinguishable from that written by humans. Similarly, the mechanical clock was first invented around the same time as double-entry accounting; today, we can send messages across the world from silicon-powered digital watches no bigger than a box of matches, and our accounting systems are smart enough to automatically code expenses with the click of a button. Technological transformation is not a new concept. The evolution of technology has shaped our world for centuries.

One could be forgiven for overlooking the changes in accounting over this period. While not as flashy as self-driving cars or autonomous flying drones, the history of accounting is as old as the history of recorded language itself; some may argue it is of equal importance. Granted, most people who would argue that are probably Certified Public Accountants (CPAs) with a vested interest in the profession. By reflecting on how far we've come since the earliest days of bookkeeping, we can better appreciate how much we have been able to automate, how much time we have been able to save, and how much further we can go with the latest innovations in technology.

THE IMPORTANCE OF ACCOUNTING

The earliest known bookkeeping records date back more than five thousand years to the reign of one of the first rulers of ancient Egypt, King Scorpion I. King Scorpion I's tomb contained numerous small ivory tablets etched with hieroglyphs that are believed to be names of ancient Egyptian towns and tributes made from each of those towns. Not only are these tablets one of the first recorded uses of Egyptian hieroglyphs, but they are also proof that keeping financial records is as old as—and inexorably linked with—the written word. In fact, many historians hypothesize that writing came about because ancient civilizations needed to record trade and business transactions.

Archaeologists have also found banking records in ancient Greek and Roman cities, where books were kept by heads of state and money lenders. These primitive records were little more than tally sheets, but they allowed early accountants to track trade and other early financial transactions.

These early financial accounting methods persisted for thousands of years as the world grew more connected and international trade began to shape early economies throughout the Middle Ages. But something was missing. It wasn't until the

European Renaissance of the 15th and 16th centuries that modern accounting was born.

The Renaissance marked a great shift in fields ranging from art and architecture to literature, politics, math, and science. In the midst of this era of expanding innovation, thought, and cultural change emerged a new accounting methodology. Italian mathematician Luca Pacioli, who is regarded by many as the father of modern accounting, documented the process of double entry accounting.

A New Era

Born in 1445, Pacioli is as well-known for his achievements as a mathematician and merchant as he is for his advancements in bookkeeping and accounting. He was a tutor of Leonardo da Vinci, and his vast collection of books included his musings on trade, profit, metallurgy, and algebra. In 1494, he wrote *Summa de Arithmetica, Geometria, Proportioni et Proportionalita*, or *The Collected Knowledge of Arithmetic, Geometry, Proportion, and Proportionality*. The book was one of the first books published on Gutenberg's printing press, an invention that paved the way for today's computers.

In this book, Pacioli included a twenty-seven page treatise on bookkeeping. Historians consider it to be one of the earliest published works that discussed double-entry accounting, which established debits and credits in every transaction. Although many are skeptical as to whether Pacioli invented this system himself—some historians place the invention of double-entry bookkeeping two hundred years earlier—his textbook encouraged its use on a much larger scale. Over five hundred years after Pacioli published his work, we still use this system to record financial transactions. Of course, where these transactions are recorded and who (or what) records them is what has changed. Through the years, changes in technology have shaped the way that we work within this system, but the system itself has not changed.

Early Technological Changes

In the United States, double-entry bookkeeping has been standard practice for businesses throughout the country's history. As commerce grew in the late nineteenth century, the need for professional accountants expanded. In the late 1880s, the American Institute of Certified Public Accountants was established, and technology continued to evolve to meet the needs of accountants across the country. The adding machine, invented by William Burroughs, allowed accountants to perform their usual calculations with improved speed and efficiency. Soon thereafter, the punch card machine of the early 1900s gave accountants a faster method for processing data. In the 1950s, General Electric purchased the first computer to be used specifically to run payroll. This technology replaced the punch card method. It is easy to imagine the excitement accountants must have felt at the arrival of this technology as they considered what it could do and what the future might hold.

Thirty years later, accountants were using spreadsheet software on business and personal computers to drastically cut the time to run payroll and keep records. As computer software continued to evolve, new applications were developed that facilitated accounting tasks. In 1998, QuickBooks—the ubiquitous accounting software still used by millions of small and mid-sized businesses today—was launched.

Customized accounting-specific software allowed computers to do more than just serve as a mainframe for data. The 1990s saw the introduction of new technologies such as Optical Character Recognition (OCR) and Intelligent Data Capture (IDC) that allowed businesses to scan and digitize invoices and other documents. By automating the most mundane and mindless tasks, accountants and bookkeepers could focus more on higher-level thinking. These early finance automation efforts led the way for the most recent advancements in both cloud accounting and ML.

We see this pattern of replacing mindless with mindful tasks continue as we apply today's latest technological innovations to the world of accounting and finance. Accuracy, speed, and efficiency continue to improve as they have for centuries. As we rely less on humans performing repetitive tasks, and shift focus to analysis and more value-added activities, we not only shape accounting but the way businesses are run in general. We already see this shift happening as companies adopt cloud accounting. Once this practice and other recently developed financial technologies are adopted as defaults, the field of accounting can continue its digital transformation.

II.

Accounting, like all areas of business, began a transition to the cloud in the early twenty-first century. Financial records were moved from filing cabinets and storage boxes to digital files on local machines, then to the cloud, which has proven safer and more scalable for most businesses than managing and storing files on an internal computer network. Accessible from everywhere and available to be backed up at any moment, the cloud has tightened security while allowing the democratization of available data within a company. This doesn't just make an accountant's job easier, it elevates everyone's tasks and time spent within the company.

THE DEMOCRATIZATION OF DATA

In the late 1990s I worked in finance for a telecommunications company. The company had a very sophisticated accounting software package which was hosted on the company's internal servers in our data center. Access to the system was tightly managed by the controller, and only a handful of accounting personnel were allowed direct access to the data.

In my role, I was responsible for reporting financial information to the entire operations department in as near real time as I was able. At the time, I was not permitted direct access to the accounting system for reporting purposes and was at the mercy of the few overworked accounting employees who had access and the speed at which they entered invoices, payments, and purchase orders. The process was inherently inefficient and introduced unnecessary complexity into an extremely time-sensitive need for information.

The company's inventory, which consisted primarily of customer premises equipment required for service delivery, was distributed in locations across the country and was managed using a Just-In-Time (JIT) process that made accurate inventory information crucial. Outdated information could lead to too few devices in one region and too many in another. Too few resulted in customer installation and service delays, while too many left inventory sitting in a warehouse waiting to be stolen, broken, or misplaced.

We had to find a way to overcome delays in the transmission of data between the accounting system, our field offices, and our vendors. Weekly reports weren't going to be sufficient for managing our processes. Fortunately, as a telecommunications company we had some expertise in data networking. Through a cross-departmental effort that involved finance, accounting, operations, and engineers, we set up a system where accounting data was pushed real time into a data lake, which could be accessed by technicians in the field. Those field technicians could see the order status of their equipment and better plan inventory levels. On the other side, the technicians could also update the data lake with on-the-ground inventory levels. By setting minimum levels for each location, our procurement specialists at corporate headquarters were able to place equipment orders in real time without waiting on a report that previously had to pass through field offices, then the accounting department, then operations headquarters, and finally to them. By making the right data available to the right people at the right time, we were able to bring our overall inventory levels down and return on investment (ROI) up.

There was no denying the fact that networked systems and a more accessible data set were improving communication and our bottom line.

No More Gatekeepers

Communications networks and cloud computing led to a paradigm shift in accounting processes. I watched as accounting professionals in my company and across the business world began to understand and adopt the usage of these new tools to improve accounting operations.

Accountants and finance professionals now had wider access to data, tighter security, and better data retention. Before cloud access, accounting software was built for individual PCs or computer servers.

Multiple users were not considered, which meant that a sole gatekeeper had access to all of the accounting data. For this reason, the changes that came with cloud computing weren't welcomed by everyone in the accounting world.

In the world before computer networks, everyone had to go to a single source for accounting information. Other departments couldn't view financial data directly. It all had to come through individuals on the finance team.

It's important to remember that, like in a democracy or other form of government, some people build power in companies by being keepers of knowledge. That's a pretty old way of thinking, but it's how many of the "old heads" in accounting felt during this shift. They no longer held the role of gatekeeper or controlled the information flow, and employees in operations and other departments were no longer beholden to them. But this mentality didn't hold a candle to the benefits that came from freeing the data.

It's hard today to imagine a company running in such a fashion, but that was the reality of the profession before the internet and cloud-based solutions. The widespread adoption of this modern approach has led to data of all types opening up to more people. The CFO or head of accounting can't act as guardians of the data now, because everybody in a modern company expects to have access to data in real time. The financial metrics that are tied to performance are key to improving that performance; the quicker the people can see them, the quicker they can act on them. Any digitally transformed company, even anybody operating on the same roles that they had throughout the last decade, expects to have democratized access to data. We can continue to expect that access moving forward without sacrificing security. This is where we are heading.

CLEANING UP AND MOVING UP

Easy access to data isn't just about who can turn on a computer and look at data. The time it takes to organize, locate, and retrieve data also maximizes the efficiency of an employee's time. Anyone who has worked in both an "old school" and "new school" office knows what I mean. Cloud computing has allowed companies to keep a cleaner virtual office *and* make room for more data and the innovative technologies that make use of that data, like AI and ML.

Businesses are built on the belief that they can provide goods or services in a better, cheaper, or faster mode than their competitors. For this reason, the primary focus is typically on the customer-facing side of the organization. A common problem for any business (but especially for startups) is that not enough attention is paid to the back-office operations. There's nothing inherently sexy about finance or accounting software, and it is generally hard to show how those functions provide value to a company's bottom line. As a result, it is not uncommon for back-office information to be disorganized and not used to its greatest extent.

I like to think of a company's data warehouse in terms of old-school filing cabinets. In a well-organized file system, company contracts, agreements, and other information were easy to find. But if there was no system in place to file the data, it could be impossible to find what you were looking for. This was important when paper files were the only way to track data, but it is especially important in the digital age.

The amount of information available today compared to the pre-digital era is greater by several orders of magnitude. But if the data can't be identified, labeled, and harnessed, it is of no greater use than those cabinets filled with paper documents. Cloud computing changed the way that we see and sort large amounts of data. If your company wants to take advantage of ML algorithms in the process of your digital transformation, you will need to get a handle on your data.

ACCESS LEADS TO AUTOMATION

Access to accounting and operational data is only the beginning for an aspiring data-driven organization. Once a company has established a methodology for data collection, the next step is to put in place ways to retrieve, organize, and analyze that data to improve operations, budgeting, sales, service delivery, and other areas of your company.

Data can come from many sources. Accounting information is just part of the puzzle. The real power of data comes when organizations can combine information from myriad sources like customer relationship management (CRM) tools, project management software, marketing lists, and inventory systems to find correlations and linkages that better describe everything from business processes to customer behaviors.

Once a company starts collecting information, the managers will inevitably strive to gather more. That is often one of the first hurdles for small or mid-sized businesses looking to improve operations through the efficient use of data.

Truthfully, most companies are not going to have access to massive troves of data that will illuminate everything about their consumers and operations. Data limitations can prevent companies from being able to make accurate predictions. The world's largest technology companies like Google, Facebook, and Amazon have gathered vast amounts of data on all of their users; that's how their analytics can get so predictive.

One example of how the huge tech companies use your data to improve their product offerings can be seen in predictive text functionality in iMessage and Gmail. If you write an email in Gmail, you can get suggestions on what to say next just by typing in a few letters. The main reason this works so well is that Google has enough data from emails that are dumped into a natural language processing (NLP) database that NLP predictors can guess what you might say next. Google's massive pile of data is so large that they can even predict information contextually. In the case of data, bigger is definitely better.

What does that mean for small companies who are trying to increase their data capabilities? Fortunately, smaller companies now have the ability to use the smaller amounts of data that they have to start using predictive algorithms and elevate the roles of everyone in the company. In Part 2 of this book, I will lay the steps to go through RPA based on limited data. Then, as the company grows and collects more data, they can actually start training ML algorithms. Cloud computing, RPA, ML, and other innovative technologies are all steps toward a full, effective digital transformation.

While cloud computing was about access, ML is about automation. A great deal of time was saved through the advent of computer technology and moving accounting from pen and paper to digital. In a truly automated modern accounting department, all manual efforts of entering invoices, reconciling bank accounts, journal entries, and accruals disappear. All of the work required to get the data into the system is done for you. ML tools can be trained to read and interpret printed documents, emails, or data that comes directly from an application programming interface (API) to a customer or vendor's network.

None of this would be possible without cloud computing and the most recent innovations in technology. Not every leader that I've worked with was willing to make this shift, eliminate the role of gatekeeper, and prioritize the "cleaning up" process of moving toward automation. But the transition to cloud computing is just another step in the journey of accounting's relationship with technology. ML is the next step for many companies and one that many have already started to take and use in their transformation. The possibilities for further elevating your company may sound just as futuristic as the printing press once sounded many centuries ago, but it's those possibilities that will bring us into the next phase of accounting and deep finance.

III.

We are already using ML algorithms, even if we don't recognize them. Let's say you make a purchase at an Exxon gas station with your credit card. Most likely, your credit card company will recognize that purchase as "travel" and use it to put together a monthly report on how much you are spending on travel. The accounting systems that small businesses use, like QuickBooks, have similar learning tools, but this is barely scratching the surface of how ML and the latest tech innovations can make our lives easier. By understanding the possibilities of this technology— not even the inner workings, but just its capabilities— everyone in finance can elevate their roles and take their job into the future.

Years after developing technology that can identify restaurant purchases as "dining" or fuel purchases as "travel," we have technology that can grab and organize this information right off of scanned or downloaded invoices. Previously, accountants would have to manually key in information from invoices: the return address, the name of the company that sent the invoice, the items on the invoice, the total, etc. All of this was recorded first on a paper ledger, and then into spreadsheet software. Accountants who have leaned into ML technology know that today's software can do all of this for the accountant, relieving them of many manual data entry duties. Of course, accountants still have to set the rules and teach the technology where the return address is located on the invoice, where the total is on the invoice, etc., but once that is taught, it can be identified and sorted. Using OCR software, all you have to do is scan a company invoice once and the technology will forever recognize how the invoice is laid out and where to grab relevant information.

Like cloud computing, ML algorithms may seem a jump too far in the future for many in the world of finance. But technology like this is crucial for an effective digital transformation. Accountants do not need to retrain in computer science to implement these tools and create a better and more cost-efficient workplace. Simply understanding the possibilities of ML will get the job done.

I have explained this to many people in finance who are hesitant to embrace the future of accounting. I tell them that failing to embrace ML is like being a race car driver and not understanding the new braking system in your car. Do you have to be able to build the braking system in order to be a good race car driver? Of course not, but if you understand the system's capabilities and limitations, you'll be able to drive more confidently and will be able to use the system to its greatest impact.

You must know the base technology the industry is using (and trust me, the industry is moving to make cloud computing and ML the "basics" of their process). Whatever role you're in, technology is a part of it and it's moving fast. If you go into a digital transformation thinking, "I'm a finance guy, and I need to stick to finance," you are missing out. If you're not keeping up with technology and you're not keeping up with the latest tools out there, you're doing a disservice to your company. Even if you're the best finance guy or gal in the world, if you're using the wrong tools, it's going to show. The future of accounting is here, and as we dive deeper into the base technology that the industry is using, you will find that you can provide more value to your team and your company.

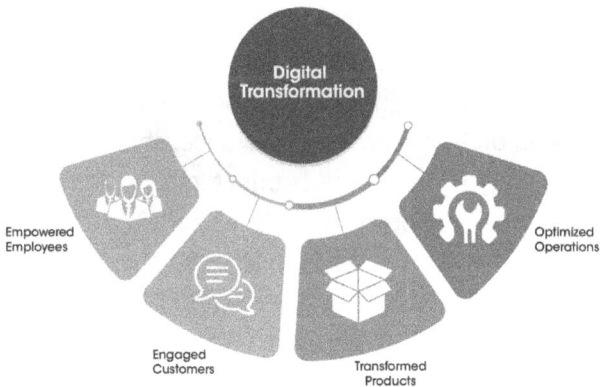

HOW DOES THIS WORK?

When employees understand the true potential of a digital transformation, they know how to make their lives easier even outside of simple data entry tasks. Instead of scouring data for trends and correlations, software that automates complex processes and monitors anomalies in real time can give employees a "heads up" on what to look for.

Let's look through the lens of a typical accounting question: why did our cost of goods sold remain the same during a period when our revenue went down? These variable costs are normally tied to revenue, but anomalies do take place. Instead of an analyst going through every invoice themself, they can spend less time working while ML algorithms spot (or even prevent) problems.

In a non-automated environment, an analyst would log in to the accounting system and pull customer invoices or sales and maybe break them down between product types. Customers may be invoiced for some bundle of software and services. The analyst would know that software products typically have a higher margin than service products, so based on her years of experience, she might start by looking to see if the product mix had changed. Maybe in the month being analyzed, the company sold a higher percentage of services than software, and the cost of goods sold remained higher because services are more expensive to offer.

In a rule-based automation system, you could program a computer to flag such an anomaly. In this example, you might program in a range that says if services make up less than 25 percent of any billing cycle, set a flag or a warning. In a rule-based system, you have to program the exceptions you want to monitor. But in a full ML-driven environment, you could run training sets based on the data you have and ask the computer to find correlations between the sets. The computer may find more examples than human eyes would have considered.

In the previous example, the answer may not have been solely based on the fact that the product mix shifted. Based on how you've trained your ML system, it may be able to detect something buried deeper in the numbers. For example, a vendor might have changed their billing rate, or maybe one of the costs was higher than usual because a single job took way more resources than a standard job. A human may be able to find this, but it would be very time consuming. Training algorithms with a complete view of vendor billing would allow the machines to identify variances more quickly than humans. This can only happen when analysts and financial teams embrace the digital transformation and understand ML systems beyond how they grab data from simple invoices.

Consider another way that automation can be used to spot trends—this time, in company spending. I worked in a business where the electric bill was a big part of our cost of goods sold. Electric companies don't bill flat rates for all users. Rates change based on everything from time of day to volume during time increments as small as fifteen minutes. When budgeting for this business, it was very difficult to forecast what our utility bill would be in any given month due to the complexity of the utility company's rate structure. ML systems could have saved me plenty of time as I tackled this issue.

Before ML, I was able to get the utility company to provide documentation on our billing by the hour for an entire calendar year. Then, I had to go back and match this to our production volume over the same time period and was then able to come up with a rate based on volume. This process took several days along with countless spreadsheets and queries.

In an ML environment, I could easily load all of the billing data, match it to the volume data, and the algorithm would find the correlations in a matter of seconds. My time would have been better spent on other tasks, and the business would have identified ways to save on their electric bill much faster.

PROVING MORE VALUE

People who study finance in school often have a specific vision for their career. They receive their degree and are excited to make strategic financial decisions for their company. They get their first job as an analyst—and then end up with mundane, data entry tasks.

This is a lose/lose for everyone. The employee gets bored because they're spending half of their workday (or more) entering data. It takes a very unique personality to be happy to do assembly line data entry and be content in such a role. Most companies are looking for people who want to grow out of that role. But with the limitations of now-outdated technology, the employer wastes money on someone who was trained for higher-level tasks. They waste even more money if the employee makes even the smallest mistakes. In accounting, transposing numbers or adding or leaving out a zero can have serious consequences. Technology has caught up to entry-level employees who spend their days slaving over a pile of invoices. What an employee with a degree can do in minutes, a computer can do in milliseconds, and with a lower rate of error. Win/win.

Here's what this might look like in your average accounting department:

Let's say a customer has a pretty standard monthly invoice rate, but it changes one month with no warning—maybe the bill drops by 50 percent. Pre-ML, an analyst would have little time to notice the change or look for a reason why this change occurred. With ML, the time a person has available because they aren't manually entering the invoice could be spent seeing if the customer changed their behavior in some way, or if it was a billing error. This kind of issue might be missed if someone is just entering invoice after invoice. But if the system flags a bill as an anomaly, the human part of the chain can spend their time managing by exception because the bulk of their time is now available for such things.

If you work in finance and want to make strategic decisions, ML gives you more time to focus on these higher-level tasks. You can start your day fresh, with data entered and ready to analyze. ML gives you the time and opportunity to provide the value you want to your company.

People up the ladder benefit, too. Not only are they saving money on paying people who aren't providing real value to the company, but their schedule becomes freed up, too. The CFO isn't in charge of entering the data, but now their team isn't, either. They now have more people on their team to analyze, talk strategy, and make better decisions for the company.

Again, I find myself explaining this concept through the metaphor of assembling and driving cars. If you can put the car together more efficiently on an assembly line, then the person who once had the job of installing door handles all day can focus on higher-level tasks. The future of accounting lets leaders use their human capital more effectively.

IT'S TIME FOR A DIGITAL TRANSFORMATION

Cloud computing, ML, and the larger concepts I will explain in Part 2 impact every area of our lives, throughout our lives. If you are my age, you remember the days when QuickBooks was first introduced, and accountants still had to work out the many kinks in the software. You might remember earlier days when it took three painstaking minutes of listening to dial-up connections to get onto the internet. In my professional lifetime, I've gone from that to gigabit fiber straight to our homes. We are still on the cutting edge of ML, but it's already started to have a big impact. If you have not yet prepared for a digital transformation, it's time.

Seeing the benefits of this technology is key for you, your team, and your company to position yourselves for implementing and staying on the cutting-edge of the technology. Even in its nascent era of the mid-90s, people understood the potential of this then-new technology. But not everyone understood what was happening when the tech boom of '99 preceded the crash in 2000. I have no doubt that leadership at your company knows a digital transformation is coming; they might not know when or how you are going to get there.

As a leader and finance professional, you know you want to be on the right side of the wave when it comes—so read on.

PART 2.

THE AGE OF ARTIFICIAL INTELLIGENCE

I.

In 1865, Jules Verne published *From the Earth to the Moon*. Imagine how extraordinary the tale must have seemed to readers whose world had been turned upside down during the American Civil War of the previous four years. The country was moving in a hopeful direction, but the transcontinental railroad was still cutting-edge technology. Affordable automobiles wouldn't be available for more than forty years. The idea of traveling from Earth to the Moon seemed centuries away, but 104 years after Verne's book was published, humans actually set foot on the moon.

Our literature and media have done a fascinating job of predicting the technology of future decades. In the 1960s, *The Jetsons* featured characters wearing smart watches, much like the ones that track our steps and answer calls for us today. Video calling has been a staple of sci-fi movies dating back to the 1927 film *Metropolis*; during the COVID-19 pandemic, video calling became a necessary part of the workday. *Star Trek* introduced the "universal translator" that allowed Enterprise personnel to communicate with aliens across the galaxy; Google Translate now lets people talk into their phones and get an immediate translation.

These items seemed far-fetched when they were introduced to popular media, but they eventually became reality. So what does that say about AI and the digital transformation of our everyday lives? Movies and books continue to predict a future where robots are indistinguishable from humans and computers are smarter than the people who interact with them. Does this mean we're on our way to falling in love with robots (like the movie *Her*), being the victims of crime-causing robots (*I, Robot*), or becoming trapped in a simulated reality developed by the AI that we created (*The Matrix*)?

These are the questions that often lie behind the fears of leaders or employees who are faced with the opportunity to undergo a digital transformation. In order to answer these questions, we must look at the rapid evolution of AI in recent decades. We have come a long way from when *The Jetsons* or *Metropolis* featured purely fantastical technology.

In my opinion, there is no need to worry about the plot lines of films like *I, Robot*. The digital transformation in the workplace incorporates AI and other innovations associated with these movies, but in 2021, they only have the capability to elevate the role of everyone on your team and increase your bottom line. Don't worry about robots taking over just yet.

THE RAPID EVOLUTION OF AI

Computers were initially built to assemble observations and perform calculations. Only large companies had access to mainframe computers, which were limited in use. But over time, the exponential growth in microprocessors has given everyone the opportunity to have a computer. The evolution of computational processing power continues to drive changes in what is possible and how portable our devices can be. Not only are computers found in every home, but their transformation has expanded to drive models that are the foundation for everything from weather predictions to epidemiology and biology.

The connection of computers has also inspired rapid changes. The internet began as networked computers mostly in universities, but as individual networks became more uniform and interlinked, we created a way for more computers to talk. This opened the door for the Information Age that we are currently living in. People are connected to virtually every other computer in the world, and we can access a vast wealth of knowledge in an instant.

This knowledge goes both ways. Consumers aren't the only people who can find answers to big questions on the web. Companies have learned to capitalize on our online interactions by tracking our behaviors, likes, dislikes, and habits. While this is mostly used as a marketing tool, all of this data is being used to train models. Big data leads to smarter computers and technology that is working through algorithms that would not have been able to run on slower computers even a decade ago.

We have seen all of this play out right in front of our very eyes: if we are not someone who remembers the days before computers or the internet, our parents certainly are. And we are also watching other innovations develop in real time. We already have Oculus Rift, deep fakes, and computer-generated speech that is indistinguishable from humans. Our journey into virtual reality will one day be completely immersive. Genetic modification, 3D printing, nanotechnology, and self-driving cars are all a reality that we are all adjusting to seeing in our supermarkets and on our streets. Billions of dollars are being poured into cutting-edge research by firms like Google, Amazon, Tesla, Facebook, Apple, Microsoft. Noted futurist Ray Kurzweil contends that most of us do not comprehend the speed of technological change. It is not linear—it is exponential. Together, we are all moving into the age of AI, where smart machines are capable of performing tasks that typically require human intelligence.

In the world of business, this is taking place thanks to a technology modeled after AI and its role in the workplace: robotic process automation (RPA).

RPA

Advancements in technology have taken tasks from individual employees, but it's unfair to say that *robots* have taken our jobs completely. When referring to robotic process automation, we say "robotic," but we're really talking about software.

RPA is a program that is configured to follow a certain set of rules that are integrated into various business systems. In this respect, RPA is very similar to a regular employee. If you hire a new employee to enter invoices, you give them a set of rules on how to do so. You show them where to put the vendor's name, how to route it, and the differences between invoices from different vendors. Not only can RPA handle these rules—but these programs will also never forget them. Instead of looking over someone's shoulder during their training period, these computer software applications have a user interface that allows a human administrator to set rules. Once the rules are set, the program captures the data, interprets it, triggers responses, communicates with the other systems, and moves it on much more quickly and efficiently than any employee could possibly do. No slip-ups or long training periods are necessary.

This is the digital equivalent of what happened in manufacturing during the last century. Very few people are still operating the machines that put together cars, appliances, or whatever is going through the assembly lines of old. No one at the factory is complaining about a bad back or how they don't want to work on Friday anymore. RPA replaced them.

I include this definition of RPA because it is the bridge between manual processes and complete intelligent automation (IA), which uses ML and AI tools. As we continue to move through this book, I will guide you from the transformation of manual processes in finance to RPA to IA.

Companies of any size can go through a digital transformation using RPA, AI, and ML. But before this happens, the company must understand the purpose of their digital transformation and where they fit in the technological evolution that is taking place all around them.

FOUR STAGES OF DIGITAL TRANSFORMATION

AI, RPA, and ML are all small pieces in the larger puzzle of digital transformation. Like any good puzzle, it must be approached intentionally and strategically. The four stages of digital transformation can lead a company of any size to a data-driven, automated workplace that elevates every person at the company and streamlines operations.

The four stages are:

- Identify and optimize your process
- Automate your process
- Use the data from that automation to further improve your process
- Monetize your process

Using your data and monetizing your processes are key steps for companies who understand the potential of their digital transformation. But the stage that is often overlooked is identifying and then optimizing your processes. Before you can automate anything and move on in your digital transformation, you have to identify and define your processes.

If you don't know what you need to automate, you can't automate. You're not going to get the results you want until you know what the result should be. So, if you're looking at getting information about your install process, for example, then you have to know what that process is. Every installer may be doing things differently, but that won't work if you want to automate this *one* process. The hardest part of a digital transformation is stepping back, looking at all of your processes, and finding the cleanest and most efficient way to perform these tasks. Only then can you automate them. We'll delve far deeper into how to do this later in this book, but for now just remember that the journey to automation begins with a slog through detailed documentation of your current processes.

Once you've documented and standardized your processes and found ways to automate your business, the real work of the transformation can begin. This is when you can begin to set up a data-driven culture, productize what you've done, and ultimately monetize your efforts. If you're successful, you can turn this process into a product to better serve your customers and stand out in the marketplace. But there is a great deal of work before your company can reach this phase. The first step is a lot of grunt work that not all companies are willing to complete. Optimizing a process drives people nuts; instead of working, every employee has to step back and explain how they work. Then different departments have to get together to talk about how their processes affect each other. It's not sexy, but it's fundamental. If you don't do this step, you can't do the rest of it.

A lot of companies *think* they've gone through a digital transformation, but they haven't completed all four stages because they still have delay points and places where data is not shared. Part of this pushback has historically come from the attitudes toward a data-driven culture, but people are becoming more receptive to it now. Data is collected in a cleaner way and people are more used to getting and manipulating data. We have all succumbed to the idea of marketers using our search histories and demographics for targeted ads. Now we also have a larger talent pool that understands what this data is capable of in the workplace. Just about any software system can export data and dump it into a database. Even if you don't have highly skilled database administrators and specific report writers, people can look at that data and manipulate it themselves without being a database SQL server guy or a full-stack web developer. Technology has come a long way, it's gotten a lot easier to use, and people are seeing the power of it, even if they're not fully utilizing it.

As little as ten years ago, this kind of digital transformation might have sounded like a direct line to evil robots and a reality out of the Wachowski minds. But along with the rapid evolution of AI came the rapid evolution of how this technology is perceived in and out of the workplace. When I preach the benefits of a digital transformation to people now, it sounds more relevant. I'm no longer speaking a different language to them. Not every workplace is undergoing this digital transformation, but for the most part, people understand what I'm saying. RPA and AI aren't black magic anymore. They are tools that can be used to completely transform and elevate the capabilities of your employees and your organization.

II.

You don't need to know how to replace an alternator to drive a car, but it helps to have an understanding of the basics of its operation before driving one. The same idea applies to the "moving parts" or pieces of digital transformations. Two of these moving parts, ML and AI, are some of those business buzzwords that everyone hears, but most people aren't actually using.

As leadership hears the stories of what AI can do, many want to understand. But it can be daunting to learn about a whole new field. There is a lot of noise about AI's immediate potential and a measure of fear about its effects. Employees, on one hand, are often scared that AI is going to take their jobs. There is also an increasing worry among business leaders, however, that if they don't learn about AI soon, they're going to be left behind or swallowed by their more tech-savvy competitors.

Not everyone has to become a data engineer, but it is important to have a basic level of understanding of the capabilities of AI and ML so that you are ready to ride the wave of technology rather than be crushed under it.

WHAT IS AI?

In 1950, Alan Turing wrote "Computing Machinery and Intelligence," in which he asked a simple question: "Can machines think?" AI is the branch of computer science that aims to answer this question by replicating human intelligence in machines. The technology that comes from AI replicates the way our brains work. Take a convolutional neural network (CNN)—a type of AI. Convolutional neural networks are frequently used for photo identification; and if you can train a CNN with enough pictures, the algorithm will be able to identify cats, dogs, or plates of food. With enough data, it can get better than people at identifying objects in images, and can do it quicker.

The intelligence comes from the way that the network scans a picture. It goes through every picture and builds one sector on another. It's a self-learning program that goes through and clusters information that it can later use to identify certain features.

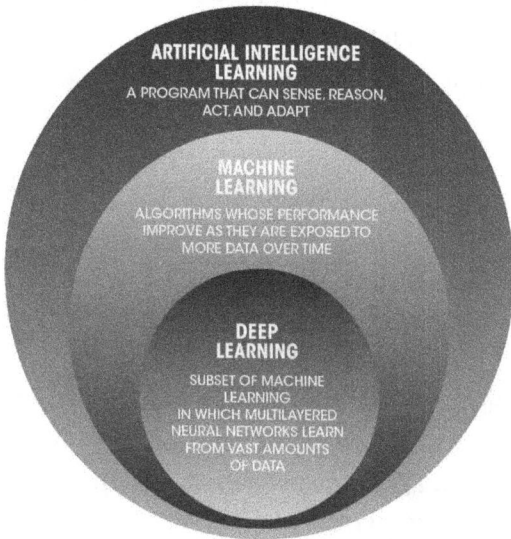

ARTIFICIAL INTELLIGENCE LEARNING
A PROGRAM THAT CAN SENSE, REASON, ACT, AND ADAPT

MACHINE LEARNING
ALGORITHMS WHOSE PERFORMANCE IMPROVE AS THEY ARE EXPOSED TO MORE DATA OVER TIME

DEEP LEARNING
SUBSET OF MACHINE LEARNING IN WHICH MULTILAYERED NEURAL NETWORKS LEARN FROM VAST AMOUNTS OF DATA

That same type of convolutional neural network may also be used for reading X-rays or identifying certain types of cancer. This sounds far-fetched, but computers are becoming more skilled than radiologists at detecting cancerous cells just by looking at X-rays.

Narrow AI versus AGI

Radiologists don't want to hear that algorithms are potentially better at reading X-rays than they are, but it's important to know that this is *all* that a particular convolutional neural network can do. The program that identifies cancerous cells is a form of **narrow AI.** Narrow AI only works in a limited context. It simulates human intelligence in one area and is only focused on performing a single task at a time.

Examples of this type of AI include:

- Google Search
- IBM's Watson
- Alexa
- Self-driving cars
- AlphaGo

These are all fascinating programs, but they can't do anything else. If AI were to have general intelligence that it could apply to solve any problem, it would be **Artificial General Intelligence (AGI)**.

To reach this level of technology that is only found in sci-fi, you'd have to have a computer that could do everything that Google, Watson, and Alexa can do *and* have self-awareness. Nobody is even pretending to build something like that right now. In 2021, engineers are all about making narrow AI as good and efficient as it can be. There have been some great technological advances in the last decade that have allowed us to add additional computing power to what we're already doing, but we're still light-years from being able to build AGI.

WHAT IS ML?

ML is a branch of AI which gives AI the ability to learn "like a human." The key algorithms and learning approaches of ML are designed to allow computers to learn progressively through continued exposure to data and refinement of the results that iteratively improve the machine's ability to make decisions. In other words, it uses building blocks of data to build a "mind" that can identify, classify, and organize different types of information.

Types of Machine Learning

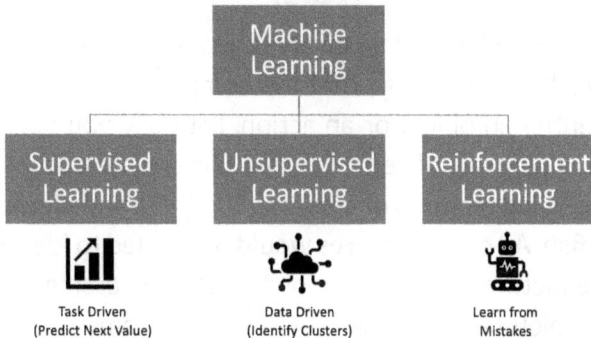

Supervised Learning	Unsupervised Learning	Reinforcement Learning
Task Driven (Predict Next Value)	Data Driven (Identify Clusters)	Learn from Mistakes

ML applications are typically tasked with one of two types of assignments: labeling something or making a numeric prediction. These are also known as *classification* (the process of separating data into multiple categorical classes) and *regression* (predicting a quantity based on independent variables).

There are three ways through which ML can train a computer in classification or regression:

- Supervised learning
- Unsupervised learning
- Reinforcement learning

Using these three forms of training, a computer can learn to take on limited skills such as navigation, making real-time decisions, or image classification. If your process contains one of these skills, you will need to recruit the right type of ML or your computer will simply fail to do what you ask.

SUPERVISED LEARNING

Supervised learning involves loading labeled data into the program so that the computer can learn to identify an object or an action. Let's say you upload a training set of ten thousand pictures of dogs, ten thousand pictures of cats, and ten thousand pictures of fish. All of the pictures would be labeled to identify the picture as a dog, cat, or fish. By processing all of the pictures with the labels the program learns to identify each picture and classify it properly.

Once that step has been completed, a second set of data containing unlabeled photos of dogs, cats, and fish would then be uploaded into the computer. This second set of images is called the **validation set**. The validation set is used to evaluate the model's performance. The computer would be tasked with identifying the animal featured in each photo.

The validation set goes through several rounds of testing with the computer. Programmers may use this set to evaluate several different algorithms. Whichever model performs the best is then selected as the model to use in the final stage.

A third set, the **test set,** is then loaded into the chosen model for final testing and analysis of the model's performance. This set contains brand new images of dogs, cats, and fish. The results are unlikely to be perfect (just search "dog" in your Apple photos app to see similar mistakes for yourself), but as these algorithms improve, so will the percentage of images that are correctly identified (or other tasks that the computer must complete accurately).

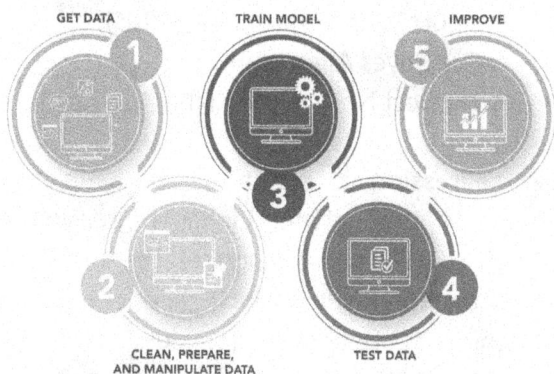

Another classic example of a widely used supervised learning algorithm is located in spam filters on email accounts. To train a spam filter, thousands upon thousands of sample emails are labeled either as spam or not spam and fed into a supervised learning model. The model identifies words, phrases, symbols, or subjects contained in both the spam and non-spam datasets and flags incoming email based on its training. This isn't perfect, but it works well enough to make our inboxes much safer and easier to sift through.

Supervised learning is the most common approach to training ML algorithms today because it is the easiest to understand and the simplest to implement. The result is a handful of algorithms that leaders can choose from depending on the data set available to them or their individual processes:

- Linear regression
- Logistic regression
- Decision trees
- Support Vector Machines (SVMs)
- Naïve Bayes Algorithm
- K-Nearest Neighbors (KNN)

Linear regression is probably the simplest ML algorithm to understand. Linear regression is a construct that lets users model the relationship between a dependent variable and one or more explanatory (independent) variables. For example, linear regression could be used to predict the price of a house based on how many bedrooms it has. If you train a model on many data points that show each variable (the price of house and number of bedrooms), the model will predict a price based on the number of bedrooms or number of bedrooms based on a given price. Of course, simple linear regression would probably not be the best predictor of home prices, as there are many other factors that impact the price of a home. These factors may include variables such as location, number of square feet, year built, etc.

Logistic regression is used to estimate discrete values (usually with a binary output of 0 or 1) from a set of independent variables. An example of a logistic regression model would be an algorithm that decides whether or not to approve a loan based on a collection of independent variables.

Decision trees are classification algorithms used to classify categorical or continuous dependent variables. Think of a decision tree as a flowchart that asks a series of questions, the answer to which produces an outcome. Decision trees are used in predictive modeling. They split data based on a set of conditions. The example below is a decision tree for rain forecasting.

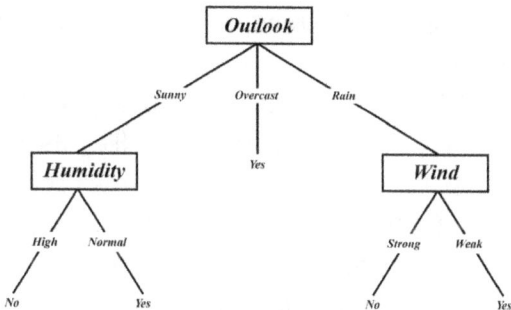

Support Vector Machines (SVMs) can be used for classification or regression. They are more commonly used for classification. SVMs attempt to divide data points into groups based on a decision boundary (called a hyperplane) that is created by a number of features. Data points are plotted in n-dimensional space, where n is the number of features included in the model. The further away the data points are from the hyperplane, the more confident we can be that they are classified correctly.

Naïve Bayes is a family of algorithms that are based on probabilities and Bayesian statistical methods to classify or tag objects. The algorithms use Bayes' Theorem to update probabilities based on prior knowledge of related conditions. Naïve Bayes classifiers consider all properties (or features) independently when calculating an outcome. These models are relatively easy to build and frequently outperform more sophisticated (i.e., complicated) models for classification of large data sets.

K-Nearest Neighbors (KNNs) can be used to solve regression or classification problems. They are easy to set up and understand, but are computationally expensive, which limits their usage in the real world. KNNs analyze data and classify it based on its proximity to other data points (i.e., its nearest neighbors). When setting up a KNN, the user defines the size of the clusters to use—for example, one model may set the cluster size at three data points, while another may break the same data set into groups of ten neighbors. In building a KNN model, the user would determine the number of neighbors to use based on testing the model's predictive abilities with different cluster sizes.

UNSUPERVISED LEARNING

Unsupervised learning is exactly what you might imagine. Using our example above, all of the dog, cat, and fish images would be uploaded into the system with no labels. The algorithm would have no basis on which to classify the data. It would instead attempt to cluster and group the images based on undefined common characteristics.

If you've ever clicked on a recommended item from Amazon, Netflix, or countless other websites, you are benefiting from an unsupervised learning model. Without being told what to select, the recommender system identifies each user's buying or viewing habits, compares them to the rest of the universe of customers, and makes a recommendation based on what customers similar to you have purchased.

I want to highlight two specific algorithms that make this type of training possible: K-means and gradient boosting.

K-means is an unsupervised algorithm that clusters similar data points. Data sets are classified into a specific number of clusters in such a way that all of the data points in a cluster are similar to one another, but different from the other clusters. Think of each cluster as a neighborhood where all of the houses are similar to one another, but distinct from the houses in the nearby neighborhoods.

Gradient boosting is a collection of algorithms used with massive data sets. Boosting is an "ensemble learning algorithm" that combines several base models to increase accuracy of predictions. While the individual algorithms may not be great predictors on their own, their power is "boosted" when combined with other algorithms. Because of the increased accuracy of combining multiple algorithms, gradient boosting is very popular among data scientists.

There are countless other ML algorithms, but we'll save those for a more technical book on ML.

REINFORCEMENT LEARNING

Reinforcement learning is much more difficult to understand programmatically than supervised or unsupervised learning. One might describe it as a similar process to training a dog. An untrained puppy starts as a blank slate with no understanding of what the words "sit," "stay," and "come" mean. It has no notion that the trash can or food on the counter is off-limits. New puppies, therefore, make lots of mistakes. When training a puppy, owners use small corrections to help it learn: admonishments for getting into the trash and treats for following a command. Over time, reinforcement models (and puppies) learn to make optimal choices.

The right type of learning for your process depends on the tasks within your process. This is just one of the reasons why optimizing your process starts with identifying the process and everything that goes into it. Once you get past this first stage of your digital transformation, you can more efficiently use AI and ML to complete tasks *for* you and your employees.

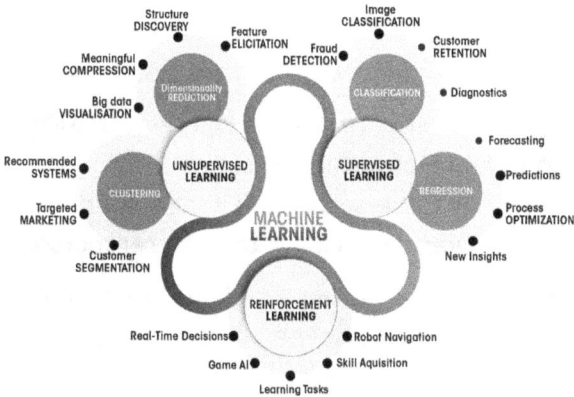

Structure DISCOVERY
Feature ELICITATION
Image CLASSIFICATION
Fraud DETECTION
Customer RETENTION
Meaningful COMPRESSION
Dimensionality REDUCTION
Big data VISUALISATION
CLASSIFICATION
Diagnostics
Recommended SYSTEMS
UNSUPERVISED LEARNING
SUPERVISED LEARNING
Forecasting
CLUSTERING
REGRESSION
Predictions
Targeted MARKETING
MACHINE LEARNING
Process OPTIMIZATION
Customer SEGMENTATION
New Insights
REINFORCEMENT LEARNING
Real-Time Decisions
Robot Navigation
Game AI
Skill Aquisition
Learning Tasks

How Has Automation Changed Society?

Automation, the umbrella term that I will continue to use to encompass RPA, different types of AI, and ML, is all around us. It follows our rules, working to help us complete the tasks that offer little value to our position or larger company.

I'm sure we've all been to a website where we've been greeted by one of those pop-up chatbots programmed to offer customer support. This is automation at work. The chatbot says, "Hi, I'm Mary, the automated helper. Please check below which area you need help with." The chatbot throws out three areas where you might need help. We all have encountered this situation, but we might not have known that this could be an application of a very simple ML algorithm. Specifically, this is a decision tree. Once you click one option (let's say you have a problem with your internet service), you move to one branch. Mary says, "What's going on with your internet service?" The process begins again: you have to choose whether your internet is slow, out, etc.

These are all just rules that will get you to the right person. Or maybe at the end of the decision tree, you can get a possible solution. If that solution doesn't work, then you can click and talk to a real person.

From a company standpoint, when you don't have to pay employees to spend however long it takes to get through these initial questions, you can save money. From a customer standpoint, they get to the right department and aren't on hold three different times until their call is transferred to the appropriate person. The customer service representative has already identified the customer's problem (or eliminated common ones) before they even say, "Hello."

When all of this works (and the company is using a well-written chatbot) the company can hire a much smaller human team. Business owners get very excited about that. If they have an existing team, they can train them to be solutions experts with higher skills.

This is where the fear starts to kick in. Yes, this also means that some job positions have been (or are in the process of being) replaced. You already know that the assembly line and factory workers of Henry Ford's time have been replaced on a massive scale by automation. Travel agents have all but completely been replaced by online travel agencies. Bank tellers and clerks, cashiers, and telemarketers all have job responsibilities that automation can assume.

But this is just the beginning. We see a lot of jobs that are at risk in the coming years. Bookkeeping clerks are at risk; you'll see why this is true in the later chapters of this book. Couriers can be replaced by drone deliveries. Proofreaders can be replaced by software programs like Grammarly and Hemingway. Analysts and researchers can't work nearly as fast as robots combing through millions of documents to find information and detect and analyze patterns and trends. Bus drivers, taxi drivers, and pilots are at risk—not yet, but this risk is on the horizon.

Many jobs, especially in the creative field, are safe (for now). Software developers are last in line for replacement. Writers, editors, event planners, and graphic designers are okay. Senior managers and business leaders aren't under threat.

Many predict robots could take up to half of the available jobs in the next two decades. Most of us currently define ourselves by our professions. What will we do in an age where the bulk of our jobs are done by robots? We've asked ourselves this question as individuals and as a society since the Industrial Revolution. Some would go so far to say that we're obsessed with this idea.

Outside of the scope of this book, what we can and must do is to put ourselves in a position where we can't be replaced by a robot or a computer program. When we in finance are no longer responsible for aggregating data, it will be more important than ever for us to be able to interpret the data and provide actionable analysis and understanding of it. This is more rewarding, but also more difficult. There is little value in entering an invoice into the accounting system, which frees us up to review and analyze invoices to ensure they are consistent. Computers can help us do this by spotting anomalies, but they can't make decisions for us. It will be incumbent on us to act on the information the computers give us.

I know that "putting yourself in a position where you can't be replaced by a robot" may seem like too simple of an answer. A big swath of society is already being left behind as automation takes over. Think about the people who used to work in coal mining or manufacturing; these jobs have been displaced and the former employees have found themselves in poverty because they haven't received opportunities to train into the solutions-based jobs that business owners seek after automating the lower-skilled ones. This book is not a political solution to this problem, but it serves to raise awareness that if there's not something to replace the jobs being taken over by automation, there will be a whole lot of unemployed people.

When this anxiety sets in, it's important to think about our transition from an agricultural economy to an industrial one a little more than one hundred years ago. The Industrial Revolution transformed the world. As farming required fewer people to produce the same yield, people moved out of the country and into the city, and the nature of the work that they did changed. The economy not only survived but thrived under this transition, as there was a whole slate of new industries and career fields that required workers. Now, many of the jobs that were born out of the Industrial Revolution are being replaced by the Digital Revolution. What will come next? We couldn't envision what jobs would emerge as agricultural jobs went away; we're in the same situation now. I think it would be irresponsible to say that this will all sort out naturally and new jobs will pop up out of thin air and be available for people who have been displaced. We need to have some kind of a plan. Otherwise, the percentage of the population that are left angry, disgruntled, and disenfranchised will feel like the economy has left them behind.

The Difference Between the AI of Today and the AI of Science Fiction

The reality is that in the near-term AI won't take our jobs—it will just change their nature. With proper planning and support, our economy will not fall to pieces. But sci-fi movies that focus on the economy would be boring. Another fear that comes with the evolution of AI is humanity itself. Rest assured, HAL from *2001: A Space Odyssey* does not exist. And he won't for a very long time.

AI today is narrow and specific to certain tasks. You can train a computer to be very good at chess, or you can train a computer to know how to handle invoices, but the program that is good at chess can't tell you what is on your invoice or what the weather is in Texas. AI and ML today are just algorithms and ways that we can use computer programs and statistics to make predictions or make things easier for us. We're a long way off from having an ethical or philosophical debate with a computer program. Human-level general intelligence is years away.

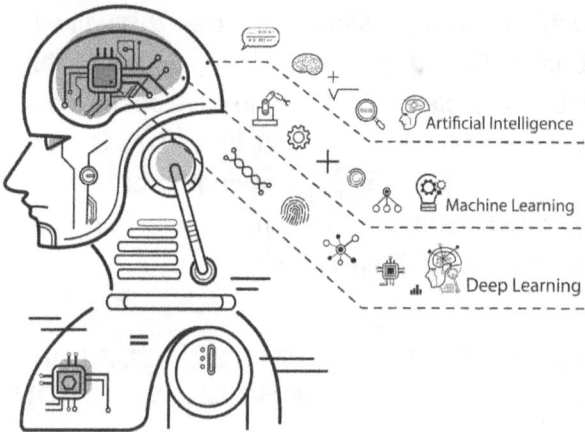

How far away are we? Lots of predictions have been made and so far they've all been very wrong. (The Amazon Alexa wasn't released until twelve years after the projected date of HAL's self-awareness). There's been very rapid progress in the field of ML, but there is also nothing to suggest robot butlers are just around the corner.

Why? Machines don't think like humans. I don't want to say they never will, but they certainly don't today. ML and AI require vast amounts of training data to do simple tasks and the ML that happens is only as good as the data given. Right now, only the companies with the most data have high-quality ML. You can use the exact same algorithms that I mentioned in this chapter—the same algorithms that Google, Facebook, Amazon, and Netflix are using, but if you don't have the data to feed them, the machine can't learn. ML that has a handful of examples cannot give a prediction as accurate as the program that has a seemingly infinite volume of data.

PART 3.

DATA SCIENCE AND LEADERSHIP IN THE AGE OF ANALYTICS

I.

Data is the fuel that powers ML. No matter how good the algorithm, ML does not work without a massive data set on which to train. Photo recognition algorithms don't inherently know how to identify dogs, cats, or fish. They must first train by reviewing thousands of images of dogs, cats, and fish.

Within this construct, the more data a company has on its business activities, the better. Fortunately, businesses across all sectors are awash in an ever-increasing wave of data that continues to increase in volume, variety, and velocity. The exponential growth of available data comes from an expanding list of sources, including traditional databases, cloud-based software systems, the internet, and social media platforms. As more businesses embrace the ever-increasing possibilities that arise from obtaining and using big data, more creative solutions are discovered and shape the future of how businesses are run.

In the last year, more than 450 billion business transactions (including business-to-business and business-to-customer) took place on the internet each and every day. Those transactions all include a treasure trove of additional data that could have been collected (e.g., time of the transaction, location of the person making the purchase, websites visited prior to the transaction, and much, much more). While the number of internet transactions already seems impossibly high, the trend has been for exponential increases with the volume of collected and stored business data doubling every 1.2 years. This means that ongoing data production today is forty-four times greater now than it was just ten years ago!

Businesses without a plan to use this wealth of data will likely drown in it.

Adoption and use of new technologies, including cloud-based accounting platforms, ERPs, ML, and other integrated process automation platforms will be integral to firms' successful use of this ever-increasing volume of customer and business data.

We just spent a long time talking about ML and the power it will bring to not only finance operations, but to every aspect of our lives. We understand the value of the data, but without a plan for how to ingest, track, and use this data it is of no use. What is the modern magic that we can use to discern the signal from the noise? How can we make sense of the infinite fire hose of available data?

Data shapes the automation that fuels digital transformations, but data alone will not solve our problems. Human experts are required to transform the data into something more meaningful. They do this using data science.

WHAT IS DATA SCIENCE?

Data science is the science of pulling information from raw data. If data is truly the "oil of the twenty-first century," then data science is the derrick that extracts it from the ether.

Data science is an important part of system automation. In fact, data is the backbone of this automation. While we can certainly link systems across our corporate network without using any of the data from each system, the real value comes in capturing the data and applying historical data (the training set) to our current data to increase predictive abilities and make use of the information we gain from each system.

If done right, data science can help banks and credit issuers identify fraudulent behavior in real time, recommend the best movie for Netflix users, and save companies millions of dollars in marketing or research and development costs. But how we get from raw data to accurate predictions or assessments requires a wealth of knowledge that is in high demand right now. Data science incorporates components of statistics, math, data engineering, ML, deep learning, and visualizations. The data scientists who can use these skills to understand and interpret data are offered high salaries for their efforts. But not all businesses even know how important these experts can be to their bottom line. In a world where the volume, velocity, and variety of data are growing every day, businesses must learn to make sense of this data to drive decisions. This requires understanding data science and building the right team to complete all of the tasks within this process.

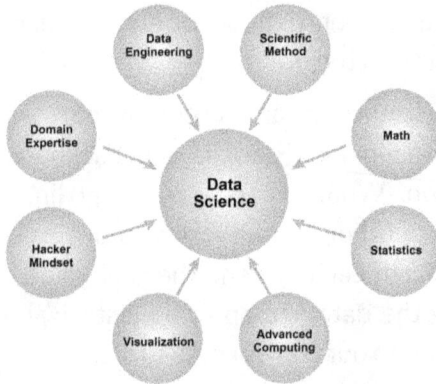

KEY COMPONENTS OF DATA SCIENCE

Data science involves:

- **Capturing data** collected from internal and external sources. Data can come from disparate sources including existing databases, websites, and the IoT (internet of things) devices such as Fitbits and vehicle navigation systems. Every day, the cookies that you accept when you enter a website contain small pieces of data. The purchases you make at a store can be collected and used as data. Businesses around the world are collecting this data and using it to fuel decisions. But collecting the data is only the first step.

- **Maintaining the data** through information governance and data architecture. Who holds onto your data after it's collected? The answer is evolving as data becomes more important to large companies and even government entities. Between Amazon's record of your purchasing history, Facebook's data on your viewing and commenting habits, and Google's information on your web history, your digital trail could be used to compile a pretty accurate representation of who you are.

- **Processing the data** through data mining, applying ML algorithms, etc. We have covered these algorithms briefly in the previous chapter. When photos of dogs, cats, and fish are given to a computer to understand what makes each of these creatures unique, the computer is processing the data it is given. When data is run through algorithms, computers can make predictions on everything from what products you are likely to buy to who you are likely to vote for in the next election.

- **Communicating results** through data reporting and visualization. Once the data is "understood," it can be communicated. These results become more and more accurate as more sets of data are collected, maintained, and processed.

- **Analyzing results** to find greater meaning. This is where data becomes most valuable. What does data say about user behavior as they are scrolling through social media sites or online shopping? What does data say about user responses to certain ads or headlines? Leaders in business can use these results to make big business decisions or just to predict where their company is headed.

Once data has gone through this process, it can be used to complete tasks that would normally take much longer and require a much larger team of analysts and researchers. Data that has been processed and analyzed can detect patterns: business direction, financial market activity, or customer churn. It can be used to automate certain processes or make recommendations on where to move the company. Or it can be used for forecasting—using historical trend data to predict future results.

These are valuable processes, spearheaded by valuable people. Knowing these people and giving them the right tasks and tools can give business leaders the opportunity to put their business on the right path and secure a strong future.

II.

Business leaders managing data science teams have to hire and interact with three main roles in order to successfully integrate data into their everyday business operations: data analysts, data engineers, and data scientists. It is important to understand the differences in these roles.

DATA ANALYSTS

Data analysts are the front-line soldiers in data wrangling. They perform specific database queries, using their abilities to gather information from disparate sources. Gathering and processing this data is messy work. Generally, 80 percent of a data analyst's time is spent "cleaning" and organizing data. "Dirty" data is nothing more than a bunch of numbers that would otherwise be useless and confusing. Someone has to go through and clean up everything. This could mean looking through thousands and thousands of observations with hundreds of different features. For example, a data analyst may receive two big data sets with a bunch of numbers that have four decimal places, some that have nine, and some that have two. Maybe the data analyst is in charge of making sure everything has the same number of decimal points so it can be processed properly. When you get into databases and queries, how you label those fields is extremely important. This is the main responsibility of the data analyst. It's certainly grunt work, but it is a crucial part of the process. Data analysts may spend a significant amount of time massaging and organizing the data before any analytics can be run on it.

DATA ENGINEERS

Data analysts aren't typically computer programmers. They don't do the modeling or build ML algorithms. This work is left to data engineers, specialists akin to data architects. Data engineers leave the stats and analysis to the data scientists and analysts. They build the tools that let these experts get to the data and integrate it across platforms. Think of data engineers as the people who identify and set up the trenches where data scientists work.

DATA SCIENTISTS

We already know that data scientists wear a lot of hats. They must be experts in math and science — including calculus. Data scientists must be experts in computer science, too. But they must also have expertise in a business or domain. Data scientists need to know the business or the field in which they are working. And, like all great businesspeople, they have to be effective communicators. Data scientists spend their days adding value to the data they analyze, so they have to be able to communicate it to the right audience(s). Usually data scientists aren't the top experts in all of the above fields, but they need to be experts in at least two and have a strong understanding of the others.

If a data scientist just had a vast amount of data, they could make some meaning out of it. If you're trying to figure out if a customer is likely to default or make a late payment on an invoice, for example, you would give that task to the data scientist. They would look at everything they know about the customer and everything they know about customers who have been late on invoices. Maybe this looks like extracting the data of every customer who has ever paid an invoice late and finding patterns or correlations that apply to all of these customers.

Using this information, they would find the best way to predict or to model the likelihood of someone being late on a payment. At this point, if you wanted to build a tool to automate this process, you would start communicating with the data engineer and they would build a reproducible or scalable application or a tool that sees what the data scientist has uncovered.

In short, data scientists leverage existing data sources and create new ones to convert the raw data into meaningful, actionable information. They are moving to the forefront of the business world. No wonder expert data scientists are hard to come by!

Data Science Venn Diagram v2.0

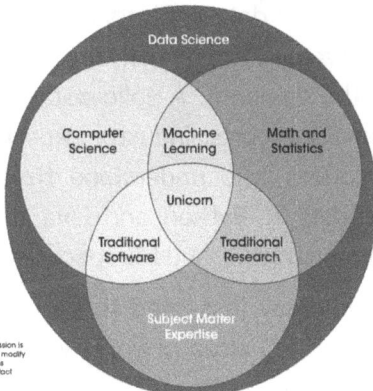

What Does a Data Team Look Like?

Data science teams vary across companies and industries. They can range from teams of dozens at large technology companies to maybe just a single person in smaller organizations. If you're only going to have one person on your team, the person you'll want is a data scientist. They will have to wear even more hats as they do the dirty work of the analyst and sometimes the work of an engineer as well. Often, this scientist will have to beg, borrow, and steal to work with the other software engineers across the company. Remember, data scientists aren't computer scientists. Many can build applications, but most are not as efficient as engineers whose sole function is to write code.

But even that one data scientist can be enough to get everyone on your existing team involved in data science. In my experience, I've been able to get company support and buy-in by showing managers what the data can do for their role and their department. If you can get a handful of people interested in what data scientists and data analysts are doing, you can slowly train a whole team to analyze data in a way that is useful to the company. A solid data science team includes domain experts, industry experts, analytics specialists, coders who understand the tools used by data scientists (R, Python, and Java, for example), database administrators, and ML specialists.

These roles may just need to be teased out of the team that a CFO already works with. Even if the unofficial data science team is decentralized, it can grow as data science improves the company's bottom line and follows growth.

Full-scale digital transformations cannot be done by one person. If you don't have dedicated resources, you will need to find the people in each department who are the most gung ho about business intelligence and analytics and get them motivated. You don't have to have data scientists in every department to transform your business and start automating processes. You just need a few people who understand the data that you have available to you and the tools that can work with this data efficiently.

Two or three people can become a full team with the right strategy and the right leader.

III.

Data scientists are the leaders of digital transformations. They turn companies into data-driven organizations by following a clear path to transformation which includes:

1. identifying opportunities (e.g., process automation),
2. gathering necessary data,
3. analyzing the data by building models and interpreting output,
4. optimizing the models, and
5. delivering results.

But they do not work alone. Data scientists are aids to leaders in top management. They give senior management the tools they need to make decisions based on available data.

In a data-driven organization, CFOs must take on a completely new role. They're not just the "bean counters" on the upper management team anymore. They are part finance guru and part data scientist.

CFOs must shift their mindset in order to keep up with the evolution of the position. This means abiding by new rules and seeing the finance role in a completely different light. Take this shift in mindset seriously, or you and your company could be left behind as the rest of the world moves forward with data science.

The historical view of the CFO as a fastidious accounting clerk detached from the nuances of operational divisions is as far removed from the reality of modern corporate finance as paper ledgers and mechanical calculators.

With the continued evolution of financial and accounting software, the nature of finance has shifted from transactional and historical to real time and analytical. CFOs are still responsible for traditional finance activities like financial planning and analysis (FP&A), audit, compliance, and treasury management, but in the era of big data, effective CFOs additionally must become masters of business intelligence.

The key to meaningful business intelligence is the effective use of data, which has moved out of departmental information silos and into the operational realm. Once considered little more than a byproduct of a company's business processes, data has become fuel for innovation and improvement.

In order to make effective use of company data, the modern CFO must understand the fundamentals of their company's business. They must be more than a financial specialist, becoming an expert at using predictive insights to harness company data to drive corporate decisions.

Finance departments have a distinct view into all aspects of the company, which puts the well-informed CFO in a unique position to combine business operations knowledge with financial insights. Further, the adoption of data analytics is a natural fit for the finance department, where analysts are accustomed to finding trends, patterns, and meaning in numbers. Similar to financial analysis, business analytics reveals trends, risks, and opportunities. With more information, analysts can use data to further refine not only financial models, but also to identify risk and regulatory issues, increase productivity and efficiency, and evaluate new business opportunities.

The following sample data science case study will help show the value of using data to drive decisions.

Data Science Case Study

Billy Ray's Soulfood Pizza Emporium

Billy Ray's Pizza is a regional pizza chain in the Southeastern United States. They have thirty-three locations in ten states, and are looking to expand into Nashville, TN. Billy Ray is not only an incredible pizza chef, he's also something of a data scientist. As such, he relies on a combination of instinct and complex data models to determine where to place his restaurants. When he goes into a new city, he looks at the competitive landscape along with customer demographic data to determine the best place to put a new restaurant. He then compares potential new sites to his existing restaurants to determine how many square feet the new site should be.

Gathering Data

Billy Ray first goes to Google Maps, and uses an API to download existing restaurants in a target city.

Google Maps © 2020

He is interested in pizza restaurants, of course, but he also wants to understand the dining landscape of the city, so he exports a list of all the restaurants.

Business Name	Address	City	State	Zip
12 South Taproom & Grill	2318 12th AVE S	Nashville	TN	37204
21 Club	1331 Antioch PIKE	Nashville	TN	37211
21C MUSEUM HOTEL NASHVILLE	221 2ND AVE N	Nashville	TN	37201
3 Crow Bar, LLC	1020 Woodland ST	Nashville	TN	37206
3000 BAR NASHVILLE	1516A DEMONBREUN ST	Nashville	TN	37203
312 PIZZA CO (CURBSIDE/DELIVERY)	371 MONROE ST	Nashville	TN	37208
312 PIZZA COMPANY, LLC	371 MONROE ST	Nashville	TN	37208
360 BISTRO	6000 HIGHWAY 100 100	Nashville	TN	37205
3701 Nolensville Rd Shell, LLC	3701 Nolensville PIKE	Nashville	TN	37211
3rd and Linsdley Bar & Grill	812 3rd AVE S	Nashville	TN	37210
400 DEGREES	3704 CLARKSVILLE PIKE	Nashville	TN	37218
404 Bar and Grill	404 Flysion Fields RD	Nashville	TN	37211

Once he understands the competitive landscape, Billy Ray wants to understand the population in the areas where he is considering placing a restaurant. He uses a combination of census data and other business sources to put together demographics by zip code.

Tools like Google Maps let him visualize zip codes in his target cities.

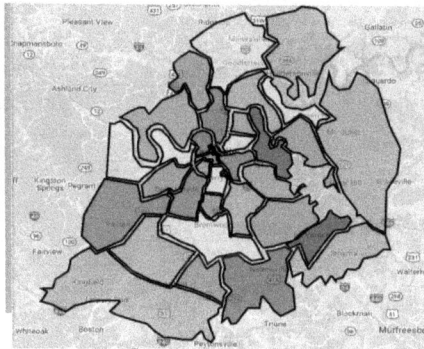

- 37214 - Donelson
- 37076 - Hermitage
- 37138 - Old Hickory
- 37206 - East Nashville
- 37216 - Inglewood
- 37115 - Madison
- 37207
- 37210
- 37217
- 37211 - South Nashville
- 37013 - Antioch, Cane Ridge
- 37027 - Brentwood
- 37220 - Oak Hill
- 37204 - 12 South, Berry Hill, Waverly
- 37215 - Green Hills
- 37221 - Bellevue
- 37205 - West Nashville

Google Maps ©2020

He uses online tools like https://www.incomebyzipcode.com/tennessee to find the median household income by zip code, and then looks at other data like population density, foot traffic, car count on roads in front of potential locations, and other demographic data such as average age, race, gender, and education level.

Income Range by Zipcode

	Total	< $25,000	$25,001 - $49,999	$50,000 - $74,999	$75,000 - $99,999	$100,000 - $199,999	< $200,000	Total Target Demographic	
37214 Donelson	16,900	3,810	5,380	3,050	1,200	1,500	200	Donelson	4,670
37076 Hermitage	20,360	6,140	5,960	3,570	1,830	2,440	440	Hermitage	9,300
37138 Old Hickory	11,680	2,410	2,910	1,970	1,200	1,650	500	Old Hickory	5,180
37216 Inglewood	10,010	3,840	2,820	1,650	670	1,300	230	Inglewood	2,990
37115 Madison	17,900	7,120	6,520	2,490	1,040	650	100	Madison	3,410
37211 South Nashville	36,110	12,460	11,270	5,510	3,040	1,370	605	South Nashville	8,350
37013 Antioch	43,070	10,760	15,390	9,890	2,930	2,840	250	Antioch	5,640
37027 Brentwood	27,920	6,110	3,260	2,820	2,120	6,830	7,460	Brentwood	4,700
37215 Green Hills	17,090	2,445	1,740	1,240	884	2,110	3,070	Green Hills	2,100
37205 West Nashville	12,380	2,960	1,920	1,800	980	2,390	1,250	West Nashville	2,380
37201 Midtown	11,300	3,190	2,770	1,550	903	1,370	1,110	Midtown	2,840
37201 Downtown	830	120	160	160	120	210	110	Downtown	350
37219 Downtown	1,240	180	200	240	170	190	100	Downtown	490
37212 Hillsboro Village	15,490	5,240	3,600	2,290	1,650	3,870	350	Hillsboro Village	1,940
37208 Germantown	6,500	3,050	2,680	1,310	480	640	300	Germantown	1,990
	247,500	70,500	66,900	35,800	20,040	28,850	19,140		55,990

Income Range by Zipcode (as % of population)

	Total	< $25,000	$25,001 - $49,999	$50,000 - $74,999	$75,000 - $99,999	$100,000 - $199,999	< $200,000	Total Target Demographic	
37214 Donelson		30%	32%	18%	9%	9%	1%	Donelson	28%
37076 Hermitage		30%	29%	17%	10%	12%	2%	Hermitage	46%
37138 Old Hickory		20%	25%	17%	10%	14%	4%	Old Hickory	27%
37216 Inglewood		29%	29%	16%	6%	13%	3%	Inglewood	30%
37115 Madison		40%	39%	14%	6%	5%	1%	Madison	30%
37211 South Nashville		34%	31%	15%	8%	6%	2%	South Nashville	23%
37013 Antioch		34%	38%	19%	7%	6%	1%	Antioch	22%
37027 Brentwood		22%	13%	10%	8%	23%	27%	Brentwood	17%
37215 Green Hills		20%	14%	11%	7%	17%	38%	Green Hills	9%
37205 West Nashville		21%	16%	11%	8%	19%	27%	West Nashville	19%
37203 Midtown		30%	25%	17%	6%	12%	10%	Midtown	20%
37201 Downtown		14%	19%	16%	12%	25%	13%	Downtown	30%
37219 Downtown		15%	20%	15%	14%	15%	12%	Downtown	23%
37212 Hillsboro Village		33%	20%	15%	11%	19%	4%	Hillsboro Village	22%
37208 Germantown		40%	28%	18%	7%	9%	3%	Germantown	31%
		31%	27%	15%	8%	12%	8%		23%

Pizza Restaurants by Neighborhood

Location	Count
Donelson	5
Hermitage	21
Old Hickory	6
Inglewood	9
Madison	14
South Nashville	20
Antioch	21
Brentwood	19
Green Hills	24
Midtown	22
Downtown	17
Downtown	14
Hillsboro Village	18
Germantown	11

Note: Some restaurants serve multiple markets

#	Zip code	Neighborhoo	Population	People/sq. Mile	National Rank
1	37212	Hillsboro Village	18,547	6,556.46	#1,154
2	37201	Downtown	1,167	3,602.97	#2,655
4	37208	Germantown	15,272	3,416.62	#2,807
5	37219	Downtown	830	3,259.85	#2,964
6	37211	South Nashville	64,753	3,030.86	#3,168
7	37203	Midtown	12,781	3,025.69	#3,172
8	37216	Inglewood	19,132	2,791.23	#3,443
13	37205	West Nashville	21,861	1,412.27	#5,405
14	37215	Green Hills	22,112	1,382.95	#5,463
15	37214	Donelson	26,474	1,260.43	#5,731

Once he has collected all of the relevant data, he is ready to let the numbers work their magic... almost. First, he has to consolidate all the data from disparate sources into a single table to make it easier to build and run his forecasting models.

Neighborhood	Population	Pop/Sq. Mile	Pizza Rest.	Target Demo	Target Demo as %
Donelson	26,474	1,260	5	4,670	28%
Hermitage	38,957	-	21	5,300	26%
Old Hickory	24,105	-	6	3,190	27%
Inglewood	19,132	2,791	9	2,580	26%
Madison	40,778	-	14	3,530	20%
South Nashville	64,753	3,031	20	8,350	23%
Antioch	86,261	-	21	9,640	22%
Brentwood	42,502	-	21	4,790	17%
Green Hills	22,112	1,383	19	2,120	18%
West Nashville	21,861	1,412	24	2,380	19%
Midtown	12,781	3,026	22	2,840	25%
Downtown	1,167	3,603	17	230	28%
Downtown	1,167	3,603	17	230	28%
Hillsboro Village	18,547	6,556	18	3,940	25%
Germantown	15,272	3,417	11	1,990	21%

Through years of experience, he has narrowed down his site selection criteria to a few key metrics. But this took several attempts, and the more restaurants he built, the more data he had to help him make effective decisions.

(For the sake of this first model, we have excluded traffic and pedestrian counts as streets have not yet been selected. This first pass model will select the neighborhood. A subsequent model will be used to pick the best street location).

Statistical software like R and the more robust Python language let him use computing power to build and evaluate models. While it is outside of the scope of this exercise, the complexities of good data models are crucial to any model's success. Learn more about model evaluation at:

https://www.datavedas.com/model-evaluation-in-r/

Once he established his model with the most predictive features, Billy Ray has used this model in each city where he opened a new restaurant.

Data Sources:

- Google Maps
- www.IncomeByZipcode.com
- www.census.gov
- www.statista.com
- www.data.nashville.gov
- https://www.tn.gov/tdot/driver-how-do-i/look-at-or-order-state-maps/maps/annual-average-daily-traffic-maps.html
- https://www.irs.gov/statistics/soi-tax-stats-individual-income-tax-statistics-2018-zip-code-data-soi
- http://zipatlas.com/us/tn/nashville/zip-code-comparison/population-density.htm

Neighborhood (adapted from zip code map), latitude/ longitude (from Google Maps), household income (from income by zip code website), traffic counts (from Tennessee Department of Transportation), foot traffic (hired local counting service).

EDA (Exploratory Data Analysis)

When the data is all collected, it is time to validate it and see if there are some key metrics that jump out before building a model.

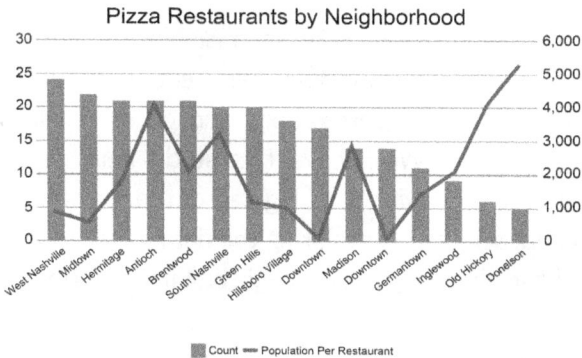

Pizza Restaurants by Neighborhood

In the above chart, we see the number of pizza restaurants in each neighborhood, and the number of residents per pizza restaurant in each area. This gives us an idea of the potential customer base and the number of competitors in each market.

We can also see which neighborhoods have the highest accessible customer base:

Target Customers by Neighborhood

Neighborhood	Target Customers
Antioch	9640
South Nashville	8350
Hermitage	5300
Brentwood	4790
Donelson	4670
Hillsboro Village	3940
Madison	3530
Old Hickory	3190
Midtown	2840
Inglewood	2580
West Nashville	2380
Green Hills	2120
Germantown	1990
Downtown	
Downtown	

In larger models, EDA is a significant part of understanding your data. Different features can be checked for correlations and other revealing information. We'll leave this study here in the interest of brevity, but a big part of the fun of being a data scientist is exploring the data to see what it tells you before you even begin building out a model.

Modeling

The first model we're going to build is one that will automatically cluster neighborhoods to help us choose the optimal restaurant location. We're going to use a tool called k-means clustering to complete this task.

Cluster Identification

Billy Ray went with fifteen clusters for his first pass on the model. He thinks, however, that he might be able to position a restaurant between two, three, or four neighborhoods to draw customers from each neighborhood, so he will use a process called k-means clustering to determine how many clusters to use, and then to cluster the areas based on geographic location (lat/long) and the other variables he has collected.

To determine optimal number of clusters, Billy Ray takes his original fifteen areas:

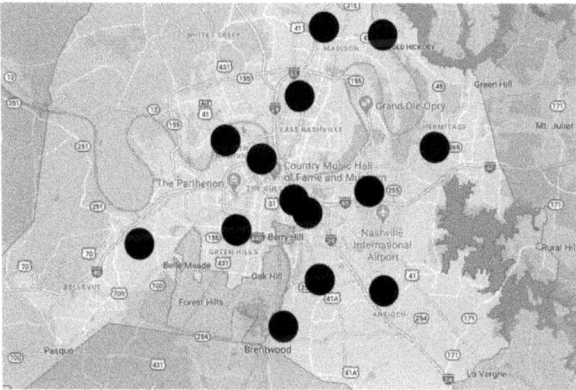

Google Maps ©2020

Billy Ray's first clusters showed him that Antioch and South Nashville were the best locations for his new pizza restaurant. Even with twenty-one existing pizza restaurants in the area, the proportion of people-to-pizza-joint is still higher than any other neighborhood.

His next step is to determine the optimal number of clusters to use for his model.

In the interest of brevity, we won't delve into the details of calculating the optimal number of clusters. We do this by calculating the error for each number of clusters.

The algorithm suggested that six is the optimal number of clusters to use based on the data we have.

Optimized map with six clusters:

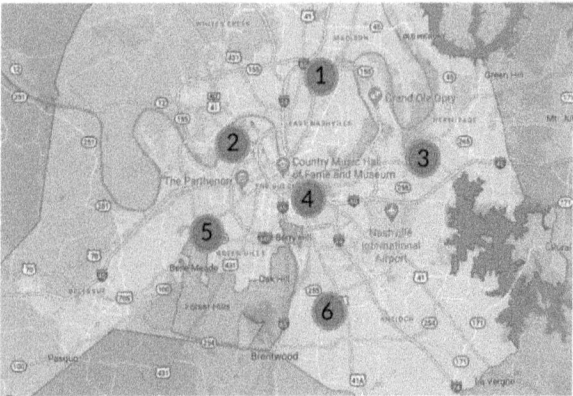

Google Maps ©2020

When we ran the model for six clusters, cluster 4 showed the optimal location for a restaurant. This location pulls in customers from three of the original clusters, has the highest population concentration with the largest group in our target income demographic, and most potential customers per pizza restaurant.

Next Steps:

With his general location in place, Billy needs to start looking at specific sites. For these sites, he will get more granular in his data and add some new fields, including traffic counts on nearby roads, number of residences in a 5-mile radius, more detailed demographic data, crime rates, average home prices, and a count of nearby businesses.

His next model will be different from the first model, which used clustering to find an ideal location for his restaurant. In this next model, he will use multivariate regression to compare specific locations to his existing stores. This will help him determine viability of a certain site and even make preliminary estimates on revenue for that location.

But we'll save that model for another day.

THE EVOLUTION FROM HUNCH TO HYPOTHESIS

Embracing digitization to increase efficiency and data availability is crucial to shifting the old school finance mindset. Historically, CFOs have stayed away from technological developments in operations, but letting this separation occur in the age of analytics can slow a company down more than a member of the finance team using paper ledgers or old-school calculators.

Embracing new technology does come with understanding and accepting new roles within the company. In addition to FP&A, audit, compliance, and treasury management, CFOs must also take on many of the roles assigned to data scientists.

This evolution has strengthened the role of the CFO. I think of this transition as going from hunch to hypothesis. The longer a CFO has been in the business world, the more they have seen happen. CFOs attain their position because they have a grasp on the history of their industry, their company, and business in general. History has always been a guide for how CFOs see their company and how they make decisions. They have seen where players on the chessboard have moved in previous games, and they know which moves have failed and which have succeeded.

But we are in the age where computers consistently beat humans at chess. So what happens when we work with the computers instead of against them? Through proper analysis of data, we can see which moves are riskier and what will affect a company's bottom line. CFOs no longer have to rely on a hunch and lie in bed at night second-guessing how that hunch will affect the future of their company. In the age of analytics, they can sleep soundly knowing that their decision is backed by data. CFOs no longer have to look backward to make a decision about moving forward; they can focus their mindset and vision on innovation, with data right by their side. In fact, this is necessary. Dwelling on the past is a hindrance to forward motion. As the CFO looks backward and waits for trends to appear, CFOs with a more innovative mindset will spring ahead of them.

When many CFOs hear that they need to embrace digitization, they may take a pause. They spent their entire career honing a specific set of skills, and now they must learn something from scratch? Don't let these fears hold you back from stepping into a digital transformation with the rest of your company. CFOs are in an exciting position to combine their business operations knowledge with financial insights. They must lead a team, which now includes a data scientist, to find trends, patterns, and meaning in numbers. Yes, they still will rely on solid financials to report on how the business is doing. But a CFO who has embraced the age of analytics will also have access to data and make predictions in real time, anytime.

If a CFO embraces analytics and understands data, they don't have to worry about falling behind, losing out to competition, or even being replaced by a robot. We're still very far from a time where algorithms are just going to replace people and leaders. Humans still have to make decisions about what to do with all of the data that has been processed. Those decisions, with assistance from the data scientist or the whole team, are often made by the CFO.

One example of algorithmic recommendations we can all relate to is the predictive text that comes up when we type an email in Google or an iMessage on our phones. Gmail and Siri offer possible words and phrases that you can choose from instead of typing out entire words. The computer doesn't always know what your intentions are, so letting it generate all your messaging on its own could be unproductive (or even disastrous). Think of leaders in data-driven companies as the person looking at the prompts and moving forward with the best choices. Algorithms offer time saving options, but the human must still monitor and guide the computer to reach the optimal output.

Neural Networks
Monthly Close RPA Transformation Data Science
Efficiency
Receivables Deep Learning
FP&A Automation Financial Statements
Data Payables ERP Artificial Intelligence Data Accounting
Digital Finance Analytics Machine Learning
Accounting Analytics Cash Flow Optimization
Financial Statements Database Automation

LEADING THE CHARGE

The proliferation and availability of business data has changed the way companies of all sizes evaluate business processes, opportunities, and threats. While solid financials will always be the ultimate yardstick on which a business is measured, there is a growing expectation that CFOs take on the role of data scientist, providing real time valuable and predictive information between monthly close reports.

The agile CFO must shift focus to where the company is going—not where it has been. Too much time looking backward at lagging indicators opens the door for more nimble, forward-looking organizations to gain competitive advantage.

With access to and understanding of consolidated data, the CFO is able to collaborate with other divisions to establish and guide Key Performance Indicators (KPIs) and metrics to connect data to core business issues. By establishing a data-driven corporate culture, the CFO can effectively drive results by leading an organization that is intelligent and responsive to data, which is used not only as a predictive tool, but as a key measurement of business success.

Effective use of big data to develop meaningful business analytics programs requires stakeholders to embrace the technologies of data science. The most valuable CFOs are those who adopt and cultivate their new supplemental role as "Chief Data Officer," taking responsibility for using data and analytics to define key metrics and provide thoughtful interpretations of data from across departments and industry.

To implement a successful business analytics program, finance departments must understand the extent of data available to the business across disparate systems, work with IT to make data available across all departments, establish data analytics and visualization techniques, and ultimately deliver actionable information to key decision makers.

USE OF TECHNOLOGY TO EXPAND CFO ROLE

The good news is CFOs are not being asked to do more with less. They are being asked to do more with more. Smart CFOs embrace technology to shift the focus of their team from transactions and reports to strategic thinking. In order to achieve this new level of business intelligence, CFOs must embrace digitization to increase efficiency and data visibility.

The first step in establishing a data-driven culture is to increase automation to let software handle back-office transactional jobs; this will allow greater human focus on strategic initiatives and advanced analytics. This may require an upgrade to the company's accounting and finance software. For those who haven't already, it is time to move away from legacy systems and a reliance on spreadsheets and adopt new technology to improve efficiency by automating the accounting process as much as possible.

Among the key benefits of finance automation are the reduction or elimination of manual business processes, reduction of data entry errors, the removal of human bias from analysis, and a move toward continuous accounting, which allows organizations to run most monthly close tasks in real time.

Not only does the CFO have to understand how this process works, but she also has to train other departments on how it works and how to properly interpret data. The CFO should be so familiar with data that they treat the data as if it's just another component of the decision-making process—another member of their team. The CFO's job is not going anywhere. CFOs will only be at risk in the future if they fail to understand how data can be used and how to interpret it to make the best decisions for their business.

THE THREE VS OF BIG DATA

Part of the mindset shift for CFOs is to truly embrace the *number* of possibilities that come with embracing digitization and big data. These thoughts never crossed the mind of old-school finance departments limited to paper ledgers and only one company's available information. Understanding the three Vs of big data can offer insight into what is possible and why it's so important to release the limits of looking in the rearview.

If you consult other experts on this topic, you might hear about five Vs or three Vs. To begin, I'll discuss the most important three and then talk about why the other two were added.

The three Vs to note are **volume, velocity, and variety.**

VOLUME

Big data isn't just called big data for no reason. The volume of data out there is astounding. Think about every computer, every phone, every connected device in your home, from your Ring doorbell to your television remote control. All of these devices are spitting out data. The automated lights in your house are spitting out data. Your refrigerator can spit out data. Every app you download spits its *own* set of data. And as I mentioned at the top of this chapter, the volume of data is exponentially increasing. When you think about the first dialup modems, you're thinking about devices that ran at fifty-six kilobytes a second. That was an okay speed for the amount of data that we were using at the time, but it had to get faster and faster as the volume of data we used increased. Now, a little more than twenty years later, we're streaming movies at home at speeds of up to one gigabyte per second! The infrastructure has to keep growing because the amount of data that we rely on for various things keeps going up. Volume is a huge part of big data. Capturing it all, to many CFOs, feels like drinking from a fire hose at the beginning of your digital transformation. There's data on anything— what will you use it for?

VELOCITY

Next is velocity. The internet isn't running at fifty-six kilobytes a second anymore. The world is moving faster than we could have ever imagined. People may go to sleep on the East Coast in the US, but they're waking up in Europe or Asia, using data on every leg of their journey. Data has to move fast to catch up and reach everybody who needs access. As we continue to build out infrastructure to carry data, we have to consider velocity. If you are trying to harness big data and learn something from it, you've got to be able to handle the volume that's coming at you and the speed at which it's coming at you.

VARIETY

The third V is variety. Data is coming from different sources: your Twitter feed, the charger you use for your Tesla, GPS information, garage door openers, you name it. There are so many different types of data coming at you. Where you used to be able to have structured databases with rows and columns, now you need significantly more complex and flexible systems. When you consider the velocity and volume of big data on *top* of variety, you may start to get overwhelmed with possibilities and responsibilities. There is a seemingly infinite amount of information coming at you, very quickly, in a variety of formats.

Those three Vs don't cover every quality of big data. In fact, the fourth V refers to the quality of the data itself: **veracity.** Is the data accurate? Is it clean? Is it worth collecting? Fifth is **value.** There is so much information out there, but does using it actually add value to your company? And when you consider these last two Vs, you can see that as smart as computers get, companies still require human input from the beginning to figure out what you can predict with the data or whether it's even useful. This is the job of a CFO or any leader who takes up the charge in the age of analytics.

PUTTING IT ALL TOGETHER

When all of this is understood and considered, CFOs can bridge the gap between finance and operations. With this bridge (built by an effective leader) comes the two-way transport of data to measure and predict performance. Better decisions are made, roles are elevated, and the company faces a reduced risk of being outpaced by innovators and disruptors in the industry.

Regardless of how big the business is, this bridge can be built and the CFO can use data science to improve the company's bottom line. The right team already exists—the CFO just needs to tap into their existing roles and offer the right tools to shift mindsets and build a data-driven company culture.

IV.

So how does this work? How does a small business embrace digitization and make the switch from spreadsheets to dashboards filled with data? Perhaps this example from my own career can illuminate what this looks like for retail companies.

I have worked in tech companies for most of my career. In that time, I've learned that even companies outside of the technology industry need to be on the front of the curve with technology when it comes to their operations. Every industry can benefit from analyzing the data that they collect every day.

Take the car wash industry, for example. Years ago, I joined two compatriots from the business world to start a car wash company. We had the belief that we could improve car wash operations by providing big business fundamentals to what had historically been a kind of low-tech "mom-and-pop" industry. Car washing might not seem like the kind of business one might think about when they think of big data, but this is exactly the point I'm trying to make.

In its early days, the company operated on point of sales (POS) systems that were not integrated across the company. Although corporate headquarters required daily reports for sales, inventory, and cash management, they didn't use these reports to their advantage. The entire process was very inefficient and fraught with potential for errors.

Each day, hourly workers were responsible for sending in the day's numbers as a part of the daily report. These workers were often high schoolers with part-time jobs, unsupervised by the company's unit managers by the time the businesses were closing for the day. Regardless of the motives of the workers, they were often distracted by all of their other closing duties. They wanted to get home—not send perfect data points to a corporate office.

The potential for ulterior motives was actually what convinced the management team to make the switch from multiple POS systems to a more automated system. When you're dealing with cash, you have to go through a long process to ensure that the right amount of cash is in the drawer. It's very easy for an employee to think that twenty dollars won't be missed at the end of the day. The few incidents of theft that I did witness turned the management on to a new system. By getting other members on board, we were on our way to establishing a data-driven company culture.

The first task at hand was linking standalone POS systems so that humans wouldn't be responsible for entering any data. No hourly workers needed to oversee sending daily reports—the system would do it all at the end of the day. Quickly, the project evolved into a complete web-based financial management tool that tracked everything from employee timesheets to cash on hand to hourly volume to the time the manager opened and closed the store. We covered everything. Part of the dashboard that employees and investors could see included an API from the Weather Channel. They could watch the weather and see the volume of sales in real time. People get hooked on this type of information. These were local investors who could've just looked out the window to see the weather outside, but they loved having it on their dashboard, and they felt we were magic for bringing this to them in real time.

The aggregated data became invaluable for operations and for our investors and bankers, who got a much better look at how the business was running. Nothing garners more confidence in those who've invested than showing accurate data on the operations of the business. Investors want to know that management has a handle on what is going on in the business. Even in down months or quarters, the data enabled us to show the variance and better explain why sales or profit were ahead of or behind budget.

Before this digital transformation, if an owner was curious about sales volume, he would drive up to each location and check things out. Afterward, I would get texts from investors on weekends: "Did you see that we washed 115 cars in Hendersonville in the last hour?" "It's going to be a great month for us with this weather." We now had passive investors who were watching the dashboard like they were watching the stock ticker go by. What more could you want out of a culture driven by data?

Extra Time to Help Out

I always say, as CFO, that my ultimate goal is to come into the office, look at some reports, make some calls, and have a workload that is manageable enough that I have enough time to sit at my desk and read the *Wall Street Journal* from cover to cover every day. I joke that that's the reason I try to automate everything. But that's what a digital transformation can do for a business, and that's what I was able to do for this car wash.

I had much more time on my hands that I could spend washing cars—literally. One day, after a winter weather event (which is always the busiest time for car washes) we had a location that was supposed to open at 8:00 a.m., but a manager arrived at the location an hour early and saw a line around the property. By the official opening time for the store, they had already washed one hundred cars. From corporate headquarters, I watched those numbers go up on our dashboard with the operations manager and the CEO. We could also see how many employees were at the location and we knew that they needed help. All three of us drove down to the unit and worked alongside the employees to keep the traffic moving. This story speaks to the power of automation for two reasons: one, I wouldn't have seen the heavy volume at the location without a centralized system; two, if everything weren't automated, there was a chance I wouldn't be able to go and help because I would be busy putting together financial reports. Instead, I just skipped out on that day's edition of the *Wall Street Journal*.

Through automation, I was also able to save time presenting to the board. The company held quarterly board meetings, and in the early days before we had linked systems and pushed real-time reporting into the cloud via a web-based dashboard, I would have to go through business volume in great detail as a part of every meeting. But after we had the centralized dashboard, I did not have to spend nearly as much time on the details because the board members were able to track company activity in real time every day through their phones or computers. They would come into the meetings fully versed in the numbers that they used to ask about in the past. They would tell us how we were doing! They'd point out patterns, telling us how rainy weekends hurt our volume and how other factors affected our numbers. We didn't have to come in and craft the whole story about why our revenue this year wasn't the same as last year, because they could go back historically and see how the weather and other factors played into the numbers.

I don't know how many of them actually visited any of the sites on a regular basis, but they all felt like they knew the business now because they had all this data. Board members and investors felt more involved with the business, even though they weren't physically there throughout the week. The more data that we gave managers and investors, the more they wanted. They were so excited that they could see sales transactions in real time. And the data was customizable by each viewer. They could run reports for single units, regions, or the whole company over customizable timelines. Investors and managers could compare wash volume for time of day, day of the week, month, season, you name it.

ELEVATING EVERYONE'S ROLE

The more data we had on store operations, the more efficient we became. And this information wasn't just available to corporate leaders. We eventually made the data available to all stores. It was amazing the impacts that democratizing the data had on the entire company. We no longer had to rely on managers to report store activities, and we could automate things like when to order cash to be delivered for each store or when to order new inventory.

We then started tracking inventory in the system and even built out a centralized ordering system, which ultimately helped us negotiate lower prices with our chemical providers. By this time, I had paired up with the operations manager, who was in charge of negotiating inventory purchases. Going up against salesmen can be hard when all you have to back up your negotiations is anecdotal reports and stories. Salesmen are better storytellers than anyone in operations. But with the right data points, the operations manager was able to talk about a vendor's product in more detail than what the vendor was able to offer. Data became a superpower for everyone in the company.

Everyone's roles were elevated—not just the people at the top. Car wash businesses are full of blue-collar workers. A lot of the managers who had access to this data were still in high school, just out of high school, or working without a college education. They were bonused based on financial performance, and I would visit them every month when they got their bonus. We'd talk about revenue and expense management. Within six months, guys who had never done so much as a personal budget were going through profit-loss statements in great detail on a monthly basis. After a few months of reviewing their store financials with them, I would get calls about the reports—**sophisticated** calls. For some of them, if I didn't know better, I would have guessed I was talking to an investment banker on the other end of the line!

It was truly a great company culture. Everything was transparent and open. While this transparency might have caused a little bit of competitive trash talking between unit managers, it also inspired everyone to achieve the right goals that were the best for the company. That hadn't happened before our digital transformation.

A Team Effort

I never wanted to be the "reports guy." I'd much rather be the guy that freed up data and let teams across the company use it however they wanted. As we saw with the car wash business, democratization of data gave everyone a greater sense of autonomy and control over their domain. It saved me time as a leader, elevated the role of everyone who worked with the data, and increased collaboration in a way that secured this new culture that the business took on.

This was a complete digital transformation of a low-tech business, and it wouldn't have been possible without data science, automation, and leadership that embraced the age of analytics.

After the transformation was complete, the car wash business was sold. When you're looking to be acquired by a larger company, you want to have a centralized system. You don't want to have messy data that a larger company will have to absorb and clean up. If you can automate like a big company, you're going to be more appealing to a big company.

The point of this story is not to brag about being part of a successful business. Rather, it is to point out the importance of gathering data and automating that process as much as possible. This is the niche I've carved for myself over the years. I help young companies (typically startups or early-stage businesses) position themselves for scalable operations that are able to rapidly bring on new customers or prepare for mergers and acquisitions (M&A) activity. Any company can do this—but it starts with understanding the basics of data science and automation and embracing how these innovations can help you through a digital transformation.

PART 4.

FINANCIAL AUTOMATION AND ENTERPRISE RESOURCE PLANNING

I.

What is Enterprise Resource Planning (ERP)?

ERP is a software tool used in the integrated management of an organization's primary business processes. For many businesses, adoption and implementation of a robust ERP system is a significant tool in process automation and data collection.

Leadership in the age of analytics involves making choices about where to use financial automation in your processes. Larger companies with an existing ERP may benefit from using automation to enhance this system. In order to make the right decisions for your team or your organization, it's important to understand the different options for automating your back office and elevating (or implementing) an ERP. We will go through the first steps of planning this digital transformation for your company and selecting the best software to build or buy. Should your company use an ERP? Is it worth looking at alternatives? How much can you do yourselves? After exploring the answers to these questions, we will look at the approach that leaders must use moving forward while working with software developers on these projects.

Before we dive into the larger ERP system and its alternatives, let's revisit the idea of robotic processing automation (RPA). Although RPAs can take place outside the world of finance, they provide specific benefits in terms of reducing errors, gaining faster access to key metrics, and making better-informed decisions for your organization. Modern CFOs should look to KPIs that let you predict the future with as much certainty as possible. RPA lets you close the books faster, shorten the sale cycle, and see earlier when expenses are getting out of line.

Back-office operations have historically been a cost center for business—meaning they cost the business money and don't add monetary value. By embracing RPA, back-office operations can take steps toward shedding that title. While there are arguments against automation because the software is "too expensive," at this point, it could be argued that the cost of *not* automating is more expensive. Sticking to manual processes will only force a company to fall behind their competitors.

Digital transformation gives finance departments the opportunity to transition from a cost center to a value center. Instead of trying to figure out how to manage costs based on mountains of invoices and receipts, finance professionals can spend their time analyzing and making strategic decisions.

RPA promises a reduction in administrative costs and increased efficiency for back-office activities. Obviously, finance managers love the idea of freeing up their employees from the mundane drudgery of repetitive tasks so they can be free to add value to the organization, but making the leap into a digital transformation is hard.

Breaking the inertia of the status quo takes a lot of effort and organization.

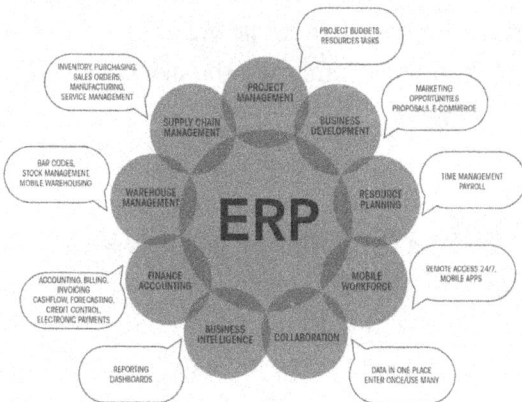

WHEN IS IT TIME TO AUTOMATE?

Although many in finance recognize the benefits of RPA, taking the leap to use it in their organizations is a different story. When is the best time to introduce RPA to your organization? If you're reading this book in 2021, the answer is right now.

About Emburse

Emburse is the world's most intuitive, trusted and powerful expense management and AP automation solution. Designed to meet the demands of today's and tomorrow's workforce, our technology empowers employees and keeps spending in compliance. www.emburse.com

---

Eric Friedrichsen, CEO of Emburse, knows all too well how the post-pandemic world can be the push that CFOs need to embrace the age of analytics and RPA. He says:

Every financial software company that replaces manual processes and spreadsheets will hit pockets of resistance from those who are happy to keep the status quo. The typical reason behind this isn't so much that they're happy with the way it's currently done—let's be honest, nobody likes doing manual processes. It's more likely the case that there hasn't yet been a "compelling event" that drives change, and therefore it's not been viewed as an urgent priority.

That compelling event can often be something unfortunate that involves a lot of pain for the CFO, like prolific expense fraud (because it's so easy to do so with manual processes) or running out of the travel budget at the end of the third quarter because you don't have accurate visibility into spend patterns. . . A more recent example of a compelling event came with employees working from home as a result of the pandemic. It quickly became clear to these organizations that the old method of sending receipts or invoices through the intracompany mail system for approval or having to go to the office to collect or mail checks simply doesn't work. Digitizing the processes in the cloud very quickly turned from a nice-to-have to a business imperative.

The pandemic also heightened the need for organizations to manage their cash more closely, particularly when it comes to the best time to pay invoices. With manual processes, it simply isn't possible to obtain the level of visibility to do this, as data is stuck in spreadsheets and is hard to analyze.

Some CFOs are hesitant to automate processes like expense management, invoicing, and bank reconciliations because they worry there will be errors if humans are not involved. The opposite is actually true. Humans are much more error-prone than computers in transferring data between systems. Automation makes it easier to detect fraud by increasing data transparency. But humans are still needed to interpret data and make decisions about the organization's direction. Automation makes life better for a CFO because she stops being a reporter of historical data and moves to the forefront as the owner of the information. This is a perfect fit because CFOs are in a position to interact across sales, operations, service delivery, etc. This objective approach lets the forward-looking CFO shape the structure of the data in the company.

If you don't adopt these new technologies, you're going to start falling behind the competition as a leader and an organization. It may be slow, incremental steps, but the further behind you get the harder it will be to catch up. You could wake up one morning and find yourself representing an anachronistic group that looks to the rest of the industry like a group of cavemen trying to assemble a rocket engine.

For the majority of firms, finance automation is still a goal and not yet a reality. The big challenge for many considering making the switch is that they don't look at it as a series of incremental steps. They are not "eating the elephant one bite at a time," to take a phrase from Desmond Tutu. (You will find that this metaphor pops up again and again as we talk about selecting and implementing software in your overall financial automation strategy).

Many leaders are taking a look at this giant "elephant" and thinking, "I'm never going to be able to eat that." But these single bites actually pave the way for larger moves and, eventually, a full digital transformation. Friedrichsen agrees:

In our experience, we've also noticed that expense is quite often the first element of a digital transformation initiative, which may also explain why it can be a heavy lift. But as a solution that touches the entire organization and is much quicker to implement than other similar solutions, expense automation can often be a great quick win for a CFO and CIO, and grease the wheels for further digitization initiatives while delighting all of the employees.

The first bite of the elephant as you read this book is to understand what financial automation and ERP can do for your organization.

What Does a Business Need?

In my current role, I must work with CEOs to understand how all of these benefits can work within their organization. When I do this, I try not to get bogged down in the technical details of pulling information into data lakes, querying systems, and choosing unique identifiers. Instead, I put together an old-school flowchart. I start with sales. What is the first initial contact with the customer? That's the first data point that will play into whatever type of RPA we implement. I map the whole customer flow through, from that initial contact to when the organization offers them solutions to the whole sales process. There are plenty of data points that can be collected along the way, and with the right automation, you can actually automatically pass that to the service delivery team, to the accounting team, or to the operations team. No one has to search and re-key all of the information.

By doing this, people can understand how easy it is to grab information from the natural customer lifecycle as it plays out in real time. If you have this for every customer, you can start building analytics around that, which could explain signs of customer churn, identify billing practices, or predict when people actually move up to a higher product. I don't think everybody has to be a database administrator or needs to understand the nitty-gritty of the details. My job is to show the value of collecting the information all along the way. You could even take that map and then mock up a dashboard where they would be able to see the kind of information that you're talking about. At some point, leaders have to make a decision about whether they want to adopt an ERP, change their current ERP, or bring in automation that can elevate their ERP. But this is another bite of the elephant.

Once the decision is made to move forward and leadership is confident in the benefits of financial automation, we can discuss the different types of financial automation. The five main types of financial automation include:

- Intelligent Routing
- Automated Matching
- Coding Templates
- Smart Coding
- Payment Plans

THINGS TO CONSIDER

- **Intelligent Routing:** Smart routing automatically directs invoices through the proper approval workflow without requiring manual inputs. Based on the information on the invoice, the system automatically identifies the correct recipient and routes the invoice for processing and coding, accordingly.

- **Automated Matching:** Accounts Payable (AP) automation should enable the use of any combination of invoices, purchase orders, receipts, contracts, or any other related documentation at the line or header level. If information is missing, the software should use ML-based recognition methods to review the document to appropriately match it.

- **Coding Templates:** Coding templates can be set up based on the vendor, supplier, item or user. Data from the invoice can be used by the system to automate the process and reduce manual intervention.

- **Smart Coding:** This next step in RPA automates coding of invoices even if they are not linked to a purchase order. Smart coding uses historical data and information on the new invoice to create coding for invoices.

- **Payment Plans:** True touchless AP systems should handle recurring payments that don't have associated invoices. These payments could be for items like monthly utility bills, rent payments, software subscriptions, and mobile phone plans. The best RPA software for AP automation should be able to identify these ongoing payments and code them properly without manual intervention.

These are specific solutions to financial systems, and there are very small differences between each. They all help to reach the same goal of finance automation: to eliminate repeatable non-value added tasks.

WHO'S TALKING?

Choosing to automate in individual departments can cut down on time and effort—until you need the automation in one department to communicate with automation in other departments. Small and midsize businesses often do not have the ability to bring in high-end developers that can make these systems talk to each other. These tools and systems are in development as demand rises, but they don't exist for all businesses right now. Market demand will drive development of these new tools in coming years.

You might have already worked with a big company that requires you to upload your invoice into an invoice tracker, where it automatically takes your information and is never viewed by human eyes. This process goes through to the payment process without being touched—it can even be auto-approved. Whether the company receives an invoice from an email, or it comes in from the mail, they just need to put it into the system and the system knows what to do with it, either through RPA or AI.

But not all leaders are willing to take that risk and remain hands-off until a cheaper solution for all businesses is available. When leaders fall into the trap of using multiple automated systems that fail to "talk" to each other, they find themselves looking for a different type of solution. Billy Hyatt, CEO of Cicayda, is very familiar with that crossroads. He says: "Automated processes alone are not the answer. We once had about fifteen different automated systems, but they did not work in concert. We dramatically decreased the number of systems and worked to integrate them. This reduced cost and complexity."

ERP may be in that strategy, making the elevation of ERPs and automation go both ways. Without automation at the top of the mind, ERP systems can require manual processes that weigh your team down and drag you behind the competition. But if you are thinking about automation first, an ERP can help you choose the right automated processes that can still communicate across departments. If you are considering an ERP or already have a system in place, you must think about where automation can help you get the most bang for your buck.

II.

ERP is a process that integrates multiple parts of a business: planning, purchasing, inventory management, finance/accounting, human resource management, sales and marketing, etc. This system covers it all, offering one centralized software for companies to complete most, if not all, of their processes.

Most ERP systems today are cloud-based and can be accessed remotely by employees. They are widely used because they facilitate communication between departments. Without ERP in place, different systems across an organization would not be able to talk to each other. With an ERP system, for example, sales orders can be connected to provisioning groups that are connected to finance. ERPs collect information from each department and make it available to other departments across the company.

Because ERPs connect different systems used by different parts of the company, they can help eliminate duplicate work, reduce transcription errors, and provide all departments with real-time information.

Some companies that offer ERP solutions include SAP, Oracle, and Microsoft. Massive teams of developers build these systems that do not have to be restricted to these larger companies. The end goal for these developers is to build an off-the-shelf solution that can be used by everyone—from Amazon and

Microsoft to restaurant chains and small businesses. The biggest challenge with building these systems is creating a tool that is flexible enough to work across any industry, regardless of what is already in place. For many developers, this requires being able to tie in other off-the-shelf systems or things the company has already built internally. One or two developers can build these systems alone. That's why, for now, it's companies like Oracle and SAP that are building and managing these massive systems.

But it's not enough for a company to use an ERP through Oracle or SAP. There has to be a person behind the ERP. ERPs are only as good as their implementation and adoption. When you're a company using an ERP at the hands of Oracle or a massive-scale company, this means that you have to be willing to change old processes in order to adapt to the ERP and take advantage of its capabilities. Often, this includes using automated processes. Before eating the entire "elephant" of adopting an ERP, companies have to take a bite out of switching over to various types of financial automation.

ENCOUNTERING AND RESPONDING TO ERP RESISTANCE

Not all businesses have embraced ERP. Why? There are two answers to this question: price and difficulty of adoption.

First, for small businesses, ERPs are still too expensive. There are no affordable ERP systems like

Quickbooks for small businesses. Leaders may want all the functionality out there, but many cannot afford existing systems, which run from fifty thousand to close to a million dollars.

For a very long time, I've been in very small companies. I have not actually been able to deploy an ERP at the company where I am now because the fifty thousand dollars required to build the ERP system would eat up a significant portion of the company's annual profits. That's really how I got into exploring ERP alternatives and trying to cobble together my own. An ERP that is close to a million dollars is more suitable for Fortune 1,000 companies and companies that have many disparate systems. These systems are so complex, depending on where they are in the evolution of the company and the automation. There could be fifty different systems, covering everything from what they use to track their customer service to the location of their delivery vans. The possibilities are endless, and this doesn't even consider the costs and labor of tying in the company's existing data.

At a million dollars, a company is getting a custom development that fits their business and processes. At fifty thousand dollars, the company is typically getting an ERP that will help link the company's existing processes together. They get a couple of training sessions on how that system works, but the client isn't high on the priority list.

Will it be this way forever? I don't think so. I think in the next five or ten years, something like QuickBooks

2.0 will come along that small businesses could actually use. QuickBooks is more intuitive than many of the ERPs on the market today (primarily because it is very limited in scope versus a full-fledged ERP system). A fifty thousand dollar ERP can be adopted, but it is going to require a lot of know-how and work from the company itself. Without analyst resources, you will have a lot of people in your company running around trying to figure out how the ERP works.

A DIFFICULT SYSTEM

Even for companies who can afford and currently use ERPs, challenges still arise. Many companies put ERPs in place before cloud computing, meaning their system architecture is tied to an on-premise system that would have to be completely reconfigured to move to the cloud.

More common than this is the challenge of working with an ERP system that wasn't fully implemented correctly. ERP systems have been around since the 1990s, and most large companies who can afford them have some type of ERP in place today, but they are routinely the source of complaints from those who use them. People think they're hard to use and not intuitive. Employees have not received proper training on the systems. This all goes back to deployment and management—unless you get everyone on board, you're going to have a hard time getting the true value out of these systems.

Maybe the vendor didn't help as much as promised, or the internal team got stuck when rolling the system out, so they never implemented fully or correctly. The cost of the ERP system alone doesn't cover all of the labor and time that goes into making the ERP system work. Most ERP systems are fairly complex and require multiple hours of training. At the end of the day, they're difficult to navigate.

ERP systems are like all software, and they will trend toward more interactive interfaces that ask plain-language questions rather than writing complex lines of code or database queries. This will go a long way to increasing adoption rates and usability of the core functions of ERP systems. But we're not there yet—not all ERP systems are intuitive.

BUILDING THE TEAM

Leaders in the age of analytics must consider who is going to undergo training and put in the labor. A full-scale implementation cannot be done by one person alone. Understanding that this task is on your list will prevent leaders from begrudging the training process.

If you find the people in each department who are gung ho about learning the ERP system, you can alleviate how much training that you have to do as a leader. Build your team, spend time with them, and let them distribute what they've learned to their teams. If you could borrow a sliver of people's time from across the organization and get them motivated, you can pull off this process without using too many resources.

Implementing an ERP system is a necessary disruption if you can afford it for your business. Setting up a complex new software system pulls people out of their daily tasks; new software deployments are never without hitches. You basically have to get everyone in the company to stop what they're doing, break their old systems, and re-create them in a new system. Whether in finance or operational roles, people are scared to change the way things work because it could have a negative impact on operations. Changes could lead to incorrect billing or worse, not delivering a product as promised to a customer. Businesses can't stop or shut down in the middle of a software upgrade, so all these changes have to happen in tandem and alongside what they're doing in their normal job. If you can't sell them on how much better the new system will be, you'll never get buy-in. ERPs are inherently complicated, and without seeing those benefits, people see them as over-complicating their lives and putting their position at risk.

All things considered, should an ERP system be involved in your next stages of planning? This depends on the size of the organization and its goals for growth. Modern ERP systems bring some basic automation and increased communication across departments, but there is still more that can be done. Evaluating your system and what solutions you need to implement can give proper directions on where and how to eat the next bites of the elephant.

Fortunately, there are some alternatives that can help companies avoid the cost, labor, and challenges that modern ERP systems bring about.

III.

Old thinking makes ERPs seem like a one-stop shop. No one ever thought to set up the sales system in a way that it could talk to the project management system or the accounting system. Everyone had their individual jobs and individual processes, much like the people in the old car factories whose sole job was to paint the car, attach the bumper, or do any other small part of the larger process.

Now, we face a new challenge. Companies have to get a handle on the data they have and find ways to make the systems that they have talk to each other. For some companies, ERPs are the solution to this problem. The system covers all departments, and everything covered by the ERP talks to each other. But, as I have already discussed, there are challenges that come with using this approach to eliminate all of the disparate systems set up with "old thinking."

Before you even think of your end result from a software level, you've got to consider your processes. Those early bites of the elephant require you to step back and look at the big picture, from the time a prospect pops up on your radar, to the time they enter the funnel, and to the moment when the deal has been closed. But don't let your process stop there. What happens with that customer? You've got to put him in the provisioning system, or the project management system, or the accounting system.

If your business is large enough that you can afford an ERP to cover all of these different systems, then you could apply your process flow and data to the ERP system. But there are alternatives to an ERP system, and these alternatives could help you avoid challenges that arise as you implement an ERP.

I understand why businesses look for alternatives to ERPs. Truthfully, ERPs are just very expensive. If you can afford it, buying an ERP is like buying everything all in one box, forcing you to move your project management system into the software, move your CRM, and spend a lot of time making that transition and learning some parts of your processes. You have to fully commit to the ERP that you're purchasing and knock out any other systems that your team members are already accustomed to using.

If you're a very small or midsize business, you may not want to make that commitment. You may not want to spend up to one hundred thousand dollars for a complete system that is going to disrupt your current processes. You may already use a number of different systems that are inexpensive, tested, and true. As developers enhance ERP systems, they may also be working on the systems that you have already implemented into your business.

Many leaders decide that instead of an ERP, they are going to bring all of their systems together and get them to talk to each other. The result is similar to an ERP—you make a cool-looking dashboard that is functional, intuitive, and easy enough for your team to use. If you have the ability to connect everything in-house, you can customize this dashboard and give team members what they want. This may be the best route for your company.

Once again, it's important to consider your budget. ERPs are expensive, but so are developers and a business intelligence team that can make your dream dashboard a reality. By the time you've hired a couple of people to put that together, you probably could have gone ahead and paid for the ERP. When you're deciding between the ERP and the alternatives, consider the price, how much customization you want for the end result, and how much time your team will need to adapt to the choices that you make.

You're Going to Face These Challenges Anyway

Every business is different, and you can't let the limitations of the software dictate what you do or don't do. If you have to build a system to meet the needs of your business, and a specific software provider doesn't have it, you're going to build it or buy it elsewhere. And now you've got two systems that need to learn how to speak to one another to keep processes smooth and eliminate the need for employees that simply act as the middleman between two automated processes. I think in an ivory tower, or in a design meeting for these big software applications, a company might claim to have a system that does everything, but businesses are going to have unique needs.

In my experience, even if somebody has gone with a more robust system, they have often found themselves building systems outside of it. When I was at a large telecommunications company located in twenty different states, their big ERP accounting system didn't fulfill the needs of the service delivery and other departments. The company needed a different customer management tool for support tickets and other systems to help the other departments. And then they faced the challenge of, despite having (and paying for) a big ERP, getting all of the systems talking to each other.

Even companies like Google or Amazon, with the development resources that they have, still face the challenges of making systems talk to each other. They could be using every single component of Salesforce or every component of NetSuite—but they're so big with so many teams that they still face these challenges. It's much rarer to find a company that has one system that actually is doing everything for them than to find companies that are scrambling to connect a big set of disparate systems. This is why even big companies with big systems have APIs and ways for these systems to have information come in from elsewhere or go out from elsewhere.

Off-the-shelf software made by big companies still has to talk to other systems if these systems are necessary to complete every process in every department. It's normal for a small company to face similar challenges even if they *can't* afford an ERP. Companies with or without APIs will need them at one point or another.

ERP Alternatives

There are methodologies and approaches that businesses can use to link their current systems without going all in on a full ERP deployment. Some of the components listed below could be used instead of or in addition to an ERP package. The right combination of software depends on your process, your company size, and how much you want to automate and manage.

Application Program Interfaces (APIs)

Everybody is building APIs these days. These tools let data flow from one system to another or to a shared database.

Think of an API as a gateway or an intermediary between systems. It allows information to be passed from one application to another. An example of an API we're probably all familiar with is when you apply for a job from LinkedIn. Your LinkedIn profile contains specific information like your first and last name, birthday, contact info, work history, etc. Some of the jobs you apply for through LinkedIn allow you to populate the job application with your LinkedIn data, which saves you from having to re-key your information every time you apply for a job. This is done via an API that maps LinkedIn fields to the hiring company's applicant database.

You can probably think of many similar examples in which two websites or systems are connected. That wouldn't be possible without an API that helps the systems talk to each other. Regardless of what platform the data starts in, an API allows you to get that data into another application. You can have APIs going in both directions, too.

While businesses might pay for certain APIs, many common ones that you might have unconsciously used while going about your day are included in software packages you already use. Another example that comes to mind is the way Quickbooks or other accounting software packages link to your bank information and automatically pull data directly from the bank.

APIs could certainly be used to connect disparate software systems your business currently uses, but in order to use them effectively someone will have to understand and architect the data flow from one system to another.

Are linked systems a better alternative to an ERP?

The answer depends on many factors. One that comes to mind is that if your business is using a project management tool, for example, that is better for your needs than one offered from an off-the-shelf

ERP system then you may not want to replace it. In this case, linked systems may work better for you.

Before you can determine the right approach, the first thing to do is look at all of your processes across the company and find the manual steps. Look at all the areas where somebody has to re-key information that's already been entered once into the sales system, the project management system, or the accounting system. How much manual rework is being done? Explore the different options available to you. You might find that a combination of open APIs and connectors is more cost-effective and intuitive than the necessary disruption of an ERP.

ERIC FRIEDRICHSEN AGREES:

It used to be a lot easier to make a business case for having a single ERP vendor for all financial applications and using their modules for all of the sub-functions like treasury, expense, and AP management. The rationale was that the process of integrating a half-dozen installed software programs from different vendors was costly and time-consuming, and updating any of the programs could lead to a number of issues. Although the ERPs modules maybe weren't as full featured as the point solution, the trade-off was worthwhile for everything to work together.

As we've moved to cloud-based solutions that integrate through open APIs and connectors, it's far easier to justify using best-of-breed vendors for each part of the finance function, not only in the functionality of the software but also the size of the company it supports.

We also find that large companies often use several ERPs across different geographies or business units, because consolidating into a single system is so challenging. These organizations are looking for solutions that can easily interface with each of them, to make life easy for both their IT and finance departments.

This focus on best-of-breed has been a core part of our approach. Instead of having one solution that tries to be all things to all people, we have a portfolio of solutions tailored to meet the unique needs of different companies (based on their size, industry, or geographical location). A thirty person company doesn't need the same solution as a multinational with thousands of employees, so it's crazy to try and shoehorn them all into the same software.

DATA WAREHOUSES AND RECOMMENDATION ANALYTICS

Data warehouses pull data from disparate systems and put them into a repository that can be queried manually through custom reports. The collected data may also serve as the source of information for company dashboards, KPIs, standardized reports, etc. Standardized reports are nice, but they don't go as far as most companies need to take full advantage of the available data. A company's ultimate goal should be to give access to all the data across the company and make it easy for anyone to pull custom reports. People shouldn't have to be experts at database queries to get these reports, either. This route should only be considered if there is an accessible way to transfer, receive, and analyze data.

Recommendation analytics can be used to provide insights on the pulled data based on data science. Although these analytics may not complete processes with the data, the results can help with forecasting and making decisions based on the data that has been collected through other systems. AI systems can evaluate dozens of variables to make predictions; but again, this data and the processes need to be identified before recommendation analytics can be used to their full potential.

ALGORITHMS AND OTHER AI COMPONENTS

The dirty little secret in today's finance world is that most finance automation is happening via RPA in all but the largest Fortune 100 companies.

Other companies are working toward true AI in finance, but it will take time for them to make this shift. There are a lot of companies out there starting to harness available data and are training their systems to recognize different parts of the process from such business cases as the way invoicing information is routed to payroll decisions to treasury management. But for now, most of this automation is rules-based and strengthens only as they build up their client base.

AI is coming in as an alternative to larger systems when prediction and forecasting are a higher priority.

We're in the early phases of watching narrow AI get better and better at what it does. If prediction and forecasting are more important for your process, this is an area of focus that could be pursued regardless of which automation path you choose.

IV.

Once your processes have been identified, you can get creative with the systems and tools that you use in your transformation. These tools may range from the simple to the complex (the most complex being a complete overhaul and the construction of a custom ERP).

What about the simplest changes? You can be well on your way to starting them right now by working with a chatbot and language processing.

Language processing is everywhere today, from virtual assistants to chatbots on websites, in the form of text or speech. This kind of communication makes it easier to interact with machines. Think of the queries you ask every day: "Alexa, what time does the sun set today?" or "Alexa, what is the capital of Pennsylvania?"

Although we often take these capabilities for granted, we can apply this kind of human interaction to finance queries. A chatbot may not completely transform your company, but it offers insight into the changes that you can make and the tools that you can use to make a difference without completely disrupting your everyday processes.

LET'S TALK ABOUT CHATBOTS

A chatbot is a computer program that interacts in natural language with humans through either speech or text communication. It uses an ML technique called natural language processing (NLP) to understand the user's intent and respond based on a set of business rules and data related to its core function.

The first chatbot, called Eliza, was built in 1966 at the MIT Artificial Intelligence Laboratory and, with only two hundred lines of code, was designed to operate as a psychotherapist.

Of course, chatbots are still not perfect, but current developments allow chatbots to improve human and computer interaction by making information available through natural language. As AI and ML evolve, chatbots will become increasingly useful. But you might not already know that they can be useful to your specific data sets.

There are two types of chatbots: rule-based and self-learning. Rule-based chatbots basically follow decision trees to respond to user inputs, while self-learning chatbots learn from interactions and increased data.

Amazon has developed a managed service called Lex that is trained on the mountains of data collected by Amazon. Lex uses deep learning to improve its capabilities with algorithms including ASR (Automatic Speech Recognition) and NLU (Natural Language Understanding). These two methodologies enable Lex-powered chatbots to convert speech to text and to recognize the intent of the text, respectively.

People are used to talking to their Amazon devices at home, but not many people actually give thought to how it works. All of the tools I have described throughout this book seem to have just appeared on our websites as we order groceries, shop on Amazon, or conduct research. We don't give them a second thought. And even though we're not thinking about it, the skills that the algorithms can handle grow every day. The capabilities expand so that we're not just using our Alexa devices to play a song on Spotify or answer a question about when our favorite restaurant is open.

These algorithms can do so much and they're so accessible. Facebook, Google, and Amazon have all made these algorithms available to us. Google TensorFlow, for example, allows you to drag-and-drop the algorithm you want to use to complete specific tasks—you don't have to be a PhD in statistics or computer science to customize your experience with a chatbot.

Relying on algorithms provided by Facebook or Amazon is an alternative (or addition) to a much larger system, but this addition has specific benefits for companies that may not have big, big data. Rather than trying to build an NLP algorithm for your company, Lex has already processed all of Amazon's data. Going back to the three Vs of big data, Lex provides significant advantages over another algorithm or tool that only knows the data you have to give it.

Amazon offers Lex for free to users, so we will be using it in this chapter to show just how easy and accessible it is to integrate these algorithms into your current processes. Lex is integrated with the Amazon Web Services (AWS) suite of services and can be implemented through a simple-to-use drag-and-drop interface. Chatbots can be deployed in just a few short minutes.

What does all of this mean for your company? The possibilities are endless. To show you just how accessible those possibilities are, let's take a look at how easy it is to use Amazon's off-the-shelf technology to build a talking, finance-enabled Lex bot for your company.

While this simple program won't replace your AP clerk, it does show some of the amazing possibilities available through readily available ML algorithms.

Building Your Own Chatbot with Amazon Lex

Setting up a basic bot

If you have never used AWS before, set up an AWS account at https://aws.amazon.com/

Click on "Create AWS Account."

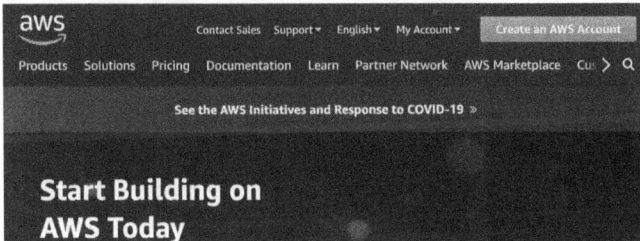

After setting up your AWS account, search for Lex in your AWS management console or navigate directly to the Amazon Lex page at https://console.aws.amazon.com/lex/

Click on "Get Started."

You can use one of the AWS templates or create your own "Custom Bot." For now, we'll create a custom bot.

We'll make one called SalesNumbers that reports our sales from previous periods.

Create your bot

Amazon Lex enables any developer to build conversational chatbots quickly and easily. With Amazon Lex, no deep learning expertise is necessary—you just specify the basic conversational flow directly from the console, and then Amazon Lex manages the dialogue and dynamically adjusts the response. To get started, you can choose one of the sample bots provided below or build a new custom bot from scratch.

CREATE YOUR OWN	TRY A SAMPLE		
Custom bot	BookTrip	OrderFlowers	ScheduleAppointment

Bot name	SalesNumbers
Language	English (UK) ▼
Output voice	None. This is only a text ba... ▼
Session timeout	5 min ▼ ⓘ
Sentiment analysis	● Yes ○ No ⓘ
IAM role	AWSServiceRoleForLexBots ⓘ Automatically created on your behalf
COPPA	Please indicate if your use of this bot ⓘ is subject to the Children's Online Privacy Protection Act (COPPA). Learn more ○ Yes ● No

(For COPPA, choose No).

Choose "Create."

You can choose a voice for speech if you want to talk to your bot. (For this first test, we'll choose text only. But feel free to experiment with speech later).

Next, you will be directed to the BotService page. From here, we will create our intents.

Create "Intent" and name it. In this example, we will create some sample intents for a couple of months with a couple of different ways users can ask the question. Here's our intent called "March."

Getting started with your bot

Welcome to your bot editor. You can start right away by adding an intent using the ⊕ button in the Intents section of the left navigation.

+ Create Intent

Components of your bot.

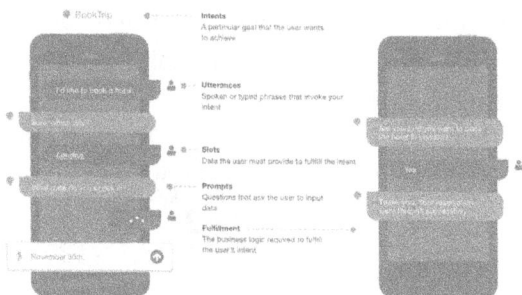

We've added three ways users can ask the question. You can add more or less.

March Latest ▾

▾ Sample utterances ❶

e.g. I would like to book a flight.	⊕
What were March sales?	✕
How much did we sell in March?	✕
What were sales in March?	✕

▸ Lambda initialization and validation ❶

Enter the response:

▾ Response ❶

| ‖ ● Message ○ Custom Markup ❶ 🗑 |

One of these messages will be presented at random.

| Sales in March were $345,218. | ⊕ |

⊕ Add Message

Press the + to add your message.

Save "Intent."

Add for a couple of other months if you want.

Build your bot by clicking the "Build" button at the top right of your screen. Wait for it to finish, and then test the bot!

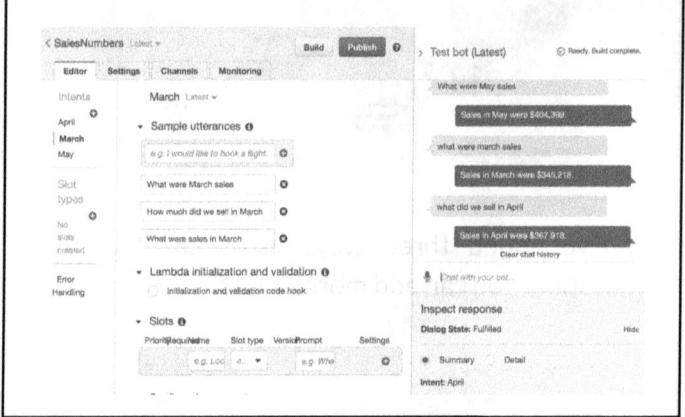

This little case study wasn't meant to show how you could replace your finance team with talking finance robots; it was meant to show you that you don't need a master's in computer science or ML to start diving into some of the concepts we've discussed.

You don't need to be a software developer to build an interactive chatbot. You, reading this book, can go out into the real world and use your knowledge of finance or accounting to create this chatbot for your organization. How cool is that?

This book primarily focuses on *leadership* in the age of analytics, but you don't have to hold the title of CFO to make this a reality for your team. People in finance spend so much of their time collecting data, cleaning data, and figuring out what to do with it. In the future, you won't have to spend your time on all of these tasks. All you'll have on your to-do list is making business decisions based on the data—not compiling the data.

The possibilities don't end here, either. Depending on how sophisticated your team is, you could have a rules-based decision tree that uses sentiment analysis to give someone different options based on the way they are typing. ML can be trained to identify typing in all capital letters as anger—it can also detect confusion, gratitude, or excitement. Not all of these tools require a software developer. As long as you are intentional with the tools that you choose and implement them properly, you can automate your processes effectively and within your budget.

V.

This case study gives a little bit of insight into how it feels to identify a piece of your process and integrate software to automate it. This is just the smallest bite of the elephant. As we lay out the options for leaders to choose, you may find yourself bouncing between two options: do you stick with a pre-existing system or build out your own?

Consider the risks and the costs of the "buy versus build" decision. These are going to be different for every organization. It would be a mistake to think you can just explain to your IT guys what kind of software you need, walk away, and wait for a perfect piece of software that works as well as your spreadsheet or word processing document. If you're going to lead and you choose to build, you need to be the architect of the project. You need to very clearly define what you need. If you've never done software development, this could be a monumental task.

But buying software is not a panacea. There are problems there as well. Before making a software purchase decision, you need to understand how it will integrate with all of your existing systems. You need to know the ins and outs of integration. Is integration included in the purchase price, or do they simply turn over the keys and wish you luck?

When weighing both of these options, never lose sight of what your ultimate goal is.

The answer may already be obvious to you based on any existing systems that you have, resources available to you, or the processes that need to be automated. If the answer isn't so obvious, consider all of these factors as you make your decision.

Comparison	Build	Buy
Time to Market	Your company is not the expert at building the type of software you want to build. If you have the resources, they can build whatever you want; but if you're not a software architect, this will be a daunting task. You will require a great deal of planning before the project is even started. As you map out this planning time, you have to ask: how long will it take to build this? What is the opportunity cost? Once it's built, you'll have to test it extensively before moving it into production. The last thing you want is for your new software to break the whole accounting process at your firm. Bug fixes and deployment add another chunk of time that you could otherwise be using training your employees on how to use an existing system that has already been tested.	The solution provider has made it their business to build solutions to do the functions you need to automate your finance and back-office operations. Bug fixes, software updates, software maintenance are handled by experts in the field. Because off-the-shelf software is not a custom-built solution, it will take some time to integrate into your system. You may need to consider additional alternatives to ERPs to bring everything together and complete all of your necessary processes.
Cost	How many developers will it take to build your software package? Is there existing staff on hand to do this or do you need to go through the hiring process in order to bring them onto your team? Again, you must ask yourself: what is the opportunity cost? What would these contractors be working on if not building your software solution?	The cost of buying an existing system can be steep because developers know that this software is in demand. Weigh the cost of the off-the-shelf software against the cost to build and maintain internally. Consider the cost in dollars *and* in time.

Ongoing Expenses	Headcount will be needed to support your software internally. They will have to monitor what happens every time you make a policy or process decision. This may result in additional development time or even additional hires. Fixing bugs, addressing crashes, and integrating your system with other systems all require time, effort, and a little bit of patience.	The solution provider handles bugs, updates, maintenance, and customer support. Consider that there is typically a fee that comes with this support, especially if it is custom to the adjustments you have made to the pre-existing system.
Employee Training	At the end of the day, who is going to use this system? They need to be trained on how to do so. What is your internal training plan? If your company doesn't develop software on a regular basis, they might not have the skills of a software development company and need to hire trainers or User Interface (UI)/User Experience (UX) people for your team.	An existing system is generally more intuitive and user-friendly than custom-built software solutions. This reduces training time, but requires that you choose a software that is intuitive and fits in well with the processes that your team currently feels comfortable with.

WHEN SHOULD YOU BUILD INSTEAD OF BUY?

Even after comparing the two options side by side, you might find yourself wondering if you should build instead of buy. But this is only the easiest answer when there is no off-the-shelf solution available. Depending on your industry, a custom solution *could* give you a competitive advantage; but as more systems are built, the window for that opportunity continues to narrow. If you do not have substantial internal resources to build a software package and can instead find an off-the-shelf solution that fits your company's specific processes, opt to buy.

If you are going to build, build one piece at a time, but don't build in a vacuum. Again, we can revisit the "eating an elephant one bite at a time" metaphor. You have to see the entire elephant first but consider where you can take your first bites. Integrate tools when free and necessary. Start small with mini apps that will eventually be rolled into the total package but can be implemented on their own at the beginning to get some quick wins. This will make the entire process much easier for your team to swallow.

When Should You Buy?

If there is already a product on the market that does what you want to do, buy. If software development is not a core competency of your business, buy. Buying increases your chances of fast deployment and implementation. Ask yourself one question before you buy: are your company's software resources better used focused on a new product or other revenue-generating products? If the answer is the latter, buy.

Internally building software may seem like a cheaper option, but you have to consider all of the costs. The time it takes to build software and the people required to do so may eat up a higher budget than buying an existing software. Maintenance also costs time and money. If you don't have the expertise internally, would it make sense to hire a software development firm to custom-build your software application?

When it comes down to it, consider the size of your software. If it's a simple and small piece of software it may make more sense to build it yourself. But if it's a large, complex system that has to operate at scale, you may be better off buying.

VI.

About FloQast

FloQast is an accounting software vendor based in Los Angeles, California. Founded in 2013, the company provides close management software for corporate accounting departments to help them improve the way they close the books each month. www.floqast.com

When Michael Whitmire, co-founder and CEO at FloQast, talks to potential customers about implementing his company's accounting workflow automation, he's confident in the time that they will have to set aside in their calendars. "Our software is incredibly intuitive because we fit within an existing process and don't ask for significant behavior change.

We have found that our clients adopt FloQast in their first month with minimal training." This process has even been done in as little as two weeks. By understanding what software and systems fit into your current processes and getting everybody on board, this fast turnaround time can be a possibility for any company looking to make a digital transformation.

Implementing financial automation, whether or not you have an ERP, will not happen overnight. It is a foundational change to the way the company works and thinks. But remember—it's a necessary disruption. Organizations that don't make the shift are going to be left behind. Making this switch is worth the initial headaches or obstacles that inevitably come with such a shift.

One of the most common dangers of implementing financial automation is overpromising. This kind of deep change takes time and may come with some bumps in the road. It is important to properly set expectations and avoid saying things that will make the rest of the management team impatient. You need to understand and champion the change while managing expectations.

A bold, brave, and smart management team has to figure out how to properly communicate that this implementation is happening, why it's happening, and what the team can do to make the process run smoothly.

PICK YOUR TEAM

We have already discussed some of the major players in a digital transformation. Potentially required roles include software developers, cloud computing specialists, UX specialists, compliance managers, and data scientists. But who is leading the charge?

The CFO is often the leader who takes the charge, as it makes sense for the CFO to oversee financial automation. But they do not have to be the person overseeing the implementation of new software and systems.

The Chief Technology Officer (CTO), for example, and whoever's running the information technology for the company, can be better suited for the position. They already know the existing systems and may have a better grasp on what systems need to talk and work together. This team knows what it means to support the systems and processes that will be elevated from a digital transformation.

The CEO needs to buy-in, at the very least. Not all CEOs will lead the charge, but they need to be a cheerleader for the implementation to go through. By the time the software is chosen and ready to implement, the CEO will already be looped into the process—someone like Michael will probably have spoken with the CEO about the transformation before anyone else.

So you've got the CEO, CTO, or CFO at the top of your list; I don't think necessarily that any of the three could do it better than the other two, but you really need to have that partnership. You need to pick a point person who fully understands the scope of the problem, what changes you have to make, and what your team ultimately wants to get out of implementing this software.

Some companies may hand all of these duties off to an outside consultant, but I think small companies can't consider this option because they can't afford an outside consultant. This isn't a problem—an outside consultant isn't going to take ownership of the project like someone from the senior management team would. An outside consultant is just coming in as a hired gun. Michael Whitmire is assured that his software works and is implemented so smoothly because it's created "by accountants, for accountants" and integrates with the client's existing ERP. An outside consultant may not be familiar with the ERP, your company, or the daily tasks of an accountant. Ideally, the person leading the charge would be someone internal.

BEFORE YOU START...

Whichever member of the C-suite takes on the leadership role has to have strong communication skills and a strong sense of empathy. This process is called a "disruption" for a reason. Leaders have to prepare their team. If you do not have an intentional communication plan ready to go, implementation is not going to occur. You'll face pushback, decreased morale, and a slew of other challenges that you do not need to add onto a digital transformation.

The message you share with your team typically sounds like this: "This implementation process is going to be painful, and we know there are going to be errors. All of the extra work upfront is going to make all of our lives better in the end."

You have to help them envision a world where their lives become much easier post-integration. If you've made it this far in the book, you already know what is possible for your company. Now, you have to communicate what you have learned to your team.

This not only includes laying out your dream for your processes, but also reassuring your team that their jobs are secure. It's normal for some entry-level workers to be worried that they're going to automate themselves out of a job. To help get them on board, you need to find ways during the transition to upskill them. Train them to provide more value to the organization. You can explain to them that you are helping them transition to a value-adding employee rather than just a button-pusher.

Clear, consistent messaging is important. Keep everyone involved updated on how the transition is going and give them the opportunity to provide feedback all the way through the process of transitioning. Don't tell employees that everything is going perfectly if it's not. Be honest with them. They will know probably better than management about all the pains of the transition because they are the ones who know the processes best. If something isn't going perfectly, arm your team leaders with a response, which would typically include an acknowledgement of the problem, a plan for how to fix it, and an open invitation for further feedback.

Be careful with how you deliver the news of your digital transformation. Have a clear path of how you inform people and who will be in charge of relaying communication to others. You're going to be battling the rumor mill as changes are made. Know what is going on and have a plan for combating misinformation. You need managers and change ambassadors to help control the message and be sure accurate information is out there to trump the rumors.

Face-to-face communication is key. People will inevitably be frustrated with all of the change going on. You can't always communicate or read emotions in email, so do everything you can to talk to employees up and down the chain of command. Use tactics like in-person conversations and "town hall" type meetings. Employees want information from the source.

This strategy is just as important as the technical side of implementing automation. Do not overlook its importance when planning your company's transformation.

THE KEY COMPONENTS OF AUTOMATION IMPLEMENTATION

Communication is key to implementing any strategy. This important factor should be considered in addition to the unique components that come with any automation implementation. By addressing implementation thoughtfully, you can lead your team through the process with minimal headaches, setbacks, and worries. Communicate all of these components to your team in order to help them see the benefits of following you through the storm.

OPERATIONAL BACKBONE

Your team wants integrated systems and processes geared toward increasing speed, efficiency, and accuracy. These systems and processes are the central components of your automated back-office platform. Keep theses end results in mind as you trudge forward.

DOCUMENTED AND SHARED PROCESS KNOWLEDGE

Understanding all components of operations of the entire finance and accounting team, the departments, and the other systems they work with is crucial to proper selection and implementation. These documented and shared processes increase transparency and lead to greater cooperation. It is important to be transparent and clear in your communication, too: you are not telling other managers how to do their jobs. You are giving them tools to better track their performance.

PLATFORMS AND DATA

Consolidating data into a single location helps your system and your team understand the core components you have to work with. This should include sales, operational, and finance data. This part is crucial to your success. You need buy-in from all departments and an understanding of how this shared data will make their jobs easier.

ACCOUNTABILITY

Who owns what? It is important to communicate the answer with other departments. They need to understand you are not taking ownership of their data or their processes. Rather, you are wrangling the data to integrate across the company to increase availability and help all departments track results. This is a democratization of data. By sharing data across the organization, each team should be empowered to track and act on what the data is telling them. Democratizing data tears down business silos.

COMBINED PLATFORM

The end goal is to create a single repository for all of the key data from your business. This can be in the form of customizable management dashboards, reporting systems, and canned reports that become part of the company's KPIs. You are developing an ecosystem where all departments share data in real time.

The hard truth is that automation doesn't come gift-wrapped in a box—or a cloud. Take small steps (and see incremental gains) but wrap them in a "moonshot project" that gets people's imagination going in the direction where you want the company to go. This transformation isn't easy—it requires a radical rethinking of how technology, people, and processes complete certain tasks.

There is no single pathway to automation. Your path will depend on existing capabilities, systems, and personnel. Communication and empathy are more important than you might think. What teammates consider a strength now may be built on later; you will need to upskill many of your employees and potentially hire new ones to help make the change. But waiting for the next step to take may leave you falling behind. Incremental changes are nice but can lead to settling for "good enough" instead of great. Think big; and as a leader, stay agile.

VII.

As you consider all of these options, also consider scalability. Can your internal application scale up? What if you start using it and it works so well that you want to use it in new and different ways? Your internal developers may have to commit more resources to account for expanded use.

Simply automating parts of your process can help you scale faster. Lost productivity from manual tasks means it will be difficult to scale finance organizations as a company grows. As Billy Hyatt says, "Manual processes are people-intensive and not scalable. You may have to start manually in the beginning, but today there are so many apps that give businesses the ability to start with automated processes. It is possible from day one to be automated."

This feels like a giant step forward, but it's one that can be done with all of the innovations that we have discussed so far in this book. Adopting AI and considering the possibilities of tapping into a data set like Amazon's make it possible to make the leap. Most leaders consider AI to be the engine that will power the next workplace revolution. Companies that don't embrace the new technology will be left behind.

Using AI to Scale

Consider the steps you need to scale your processes. AI can help you get there. Relying on AI can decrease costs, increase productivity, and allow your company to increase customer focus. AI can support your team through various tasks, including data processing, creating reports, and discovering trends that your team can later use to make decisions moving forward. With AI doing all of the tedious work, you can spend more time training your team to take on higher-level tasks. AI can act as an entire army of analysts and data entry specialists, scaling as large as you need, when you need it. When its power is recognized by leaders, AI can be a champion in your organization and scaling efforts.

Like implementing an ERP system or new software, implementing AI takes time and requires clear intent. Time will need to be set aside to train employees. Strategic initiatives must be developed to determine where AI can help scale your organization. In-house and third-party solutions can help you through this development. But like software, the costs of using AI don't have to outweigh the benefits. AI might be the final piece of the puzzle for scaling your processes.

USING DATA TO SCALE

Meanwhile, there are other data initiatives that can be used to propel your company forward. You can use data and analytics to improve current processes, leverage data and analytics for reporting and/ or product improvement, or focus on data-driven decision making. Your team no longer has to make decisions based on a "hunch." They can use data to drive every decision and guide others on how to make these decisions as well.

All of the structured relational data from your existing systems, documents, images, text, and audio can be used in initiatives right now. But be intentional. Most people don't even know what their data needs are until they have gone through the process of identifying their processes and automating. You must understand this completely before embarking on a true digital transformation.

The needed data must be identified before it can be gathered; many companies run into a wall because they have a lack of curated data to train systems, compounded by a lack of a data governance strategy. Finance must work with IT and other groups to put this in place. Data must be connected internally and externally. Every step of this process must be planned out in order to reduce problems, save time, and use resources effectively.

VIII.

For the leaders who are looking to develop software in-house, part of your job is to plan your approach to development. This approach has changed in a way that allows companies to adjust to changing needs and focus on individual tasks as they come up. Technology is changing so fast that leaders need to be agile.

For nearly two decades, developers have been refining and improving the Agile software development process, which has since been expanded to be a methodology not just for software development, but for project management in general.

There are entire books on Agile development, so we will not reinvent the wheel here. This novel approach to software development and project management is important, however. I'm used to enough success in prior digital transformations that it's worth diving into a little bit in the coming pages.

Here's what it means to "be" Agile.

THE AGILE MANIFESTO

Agile methodology is a project management process that is based on collaborative interaction between self-organizing teams that interact with "customers," who are the people for whom the software is being developed.

The Agile Manifesto, published in 2001, marked a turning point in how developers and business leaders approached software development together. This manifesto covered four values and twelve principles that most software developers adhere to today:

Values

- Individuals and interactions over processes and tools
- Working software over comprehensive documentation
- Customer collaboration over contract negotiation
- Responding to change over following a plan

Principles

- Customer satisfaction through early and continuous software delivery

- Accommodate changing requirements throughout the development process
- Frequent delivery of working software
- Collaboration between the business stakeholders and developers throughout the project
- Support, trust, and motivate the people involved
- Enable face-to-face interactions
- Working software is the primary measure of progress
- Agile processes to support a consistent development pace
- Attention to technical detail and design enhances agility
- Simplicity
- Self-organizing teams encourage great architectures, requirements, and designs
- Regular reflections on how to become more effective

Sticking to these values and principles will help you work through any project with software developers, whether you decide to build or buy, scale or stay small.

What Is Agile?

Agile development was created as an alternative approach to software development that differs greatly from the old-school approach. The "old-school" approach, Waterfall, is a development plan that writes one line of code at a time. After the code is written, everyone involved sits down and tries to imagine all of the hypotheticals that come with that one line of code. You're picturing something that doesn't exist, and then you're building hypothetical layers on it. Before you even build a base product, you're trying to build out the end-all, be-all solution of a finished product.

If the Waterfall approach was used to build a house, the homeowner would tell the architect everything that they wanted in a house all at once: twelve-foot ceilings, a three-car garage, a kitchen on the second floor, etc. Avid viewers of home renovation shows know that this approach doesn't always work out. Problems come up as the house is being built; structural issues prevent the homeowner from getting everything they want. The homeowner ends up disappointed at the end of the process.

Agile approaches software development differently. The "architect" in the home building metaphor sketches out all of the homeowner's demands, piece by piece. They can spot problems as they arise and ask the homeowner to adjust, compromise, or brainstorm alternative ideas for the end result. The person in this metaphor acting as the homeowner is not a software developer. They're going to be the user of the product—the leader of the business or the team that will engage with its processes every day. These "homeowners" may know what they want, but they don't know the limitations of software and what may not be possible. Only through working with the architect (or software developer), piece by piece, can both parties manage expectations and create a usable, satisfying end result.

The great thing about Agile is that it forces constant back-and-forth communication between the developers and their customers. In my role, my customers are the leaders who are trying to build or buy the right software for their company. Software developers have a similar relationship. Their customer is whatever department needs this tool. Using an Agile approach, we all work together to create the right "elephant," one bite at a time.

In Agile programming, the first thing you do is write stories. No one has to get technical and pick out whether they want a tool in JavaScript or Python. The story writing just builds out what tools will accomplish certain tasks. Once this story is written, the customer sits down with the lead developer and they have a conversation about the specifics of what the customer is envisioning. The lead developer will then go back and figure out what technology is best to use.

If you're building Zoom, one story might sound like this: "Ok, we need a camera interface. We need a microphone interface. The main screen will have X, Y, and Z capabilities. The chat will have X, Y, and Z capabilities."

Each of these features tells a different story. Instead of going out, trying to build it all at once, and then coming back, and depending on the size of your development team, the Agile approach gives the developer the opportunity to choose one person to work on the audio integration, one person to work on video integration, one person to work on the chat, etc. During this time, the customer has meetings with the development team and sees the results as they roll out. The customer can test each component of the end result before the ultimate delivery.

When you're doing large-scale automation, having that feedback can prevent so many problems which could ultimately require unraveling all of the work done on a project. If you have to wait until the end of the project to find out that you haven't met the customer's vision, you have a lot of work ahead of you.

The Agile approach is much more nimble than Waterfall. Both approaches start with the end in mind, but the way you get there with Agile is much more interactive. There could be so many changes that, ultimately, what you end up with isn't what was defined on day one but is still satisfying to the customer. Iteratively building a product rather than building it in a vacuum produces a better product and everybody's on the same page throughout the whole process.

This is the approach that leaders will need to take as they move forward with the strategy that they have built for their digital transformation. Once software has been chosen (or a leader has chosen to build), it's time to reach out to a software developer and be Agile.

PART 5.

THE FINANCE
AUTOMATION TEAM

I.

The general rules of finance and accounting are pretty consistent. The consistency principle is actually one of the basic tenets of financial reporting: once an accounting method or principle has been chosen, it should be followed throughout all accounting periods. So it is easy to see why change can be hard for accountants and finance professionals. Changes in processes and procedures could have impacts on the reporting of financial results, which could cause concern for company managers and investors. But agile finance teams have to be careful not to fall into the rut of following standard processes without ever questioning when, why, or how they're done. If the finance team has been following the same process for years, they are likely to fall behind the competition. They are not well-positioned to bring any new value to the organization.

This is part of the reason I ended up taking a coding class after twenty years of working in finance.

I got my MBA in the late 90s, and coding definitely wasn't part of the curriculum back then. I was only interested in it because I was (and remain) a bit of a nerd. Also, the "coding" I did back then wasn't terribly advanced: I knew how to build websites with HTML and a little JavaScript, but not much more.

This little bit of knowledge served me well as I moved through my career and more and more of the work finance departments were moving to the cloud. At one point in the early 2000s I was spending more time building out web-based KPI dashboards than actually working on the financial reports. What started as a niche became the impetus that drove my professional trajectory toward working on finance automation for the next two decades.

A lifelong learner, a few years ago I decided to go back to school for a second master's degree (this one in finance). While I had worked in finance for years before going back to school, and I thought I'd done a pretty good job keeping up with the latest industry tech, I was very happy to be exposed to a whole new level of tools of the trade.

My first exposure to the new computer science-driven world of finance was in a statistics course, where instead of using a calculator, we started using a software application called RStudio. R is a statistics-based programming language, but it's also a "gateway drug" into much more serious programming. It's the only gateway drug I recommend to CFOs, and it was an eye-opening experience for me. Once you learn how to use it, you will see how much you can do with the massive amounts of data available to you.

I call R a gateway drug because it gives you enough tools to be dangerous, but once you become proficient you start looking for a broader toolset that will let you do even more with the data. Soon you find yourself studying Python and downloading NumPy, pandas, and other data science libraries, jonesing for your next data fix!

If you're not changing and evolving as a professional (or as a company), you're going to be left behind. You're going to get replaced. Old-school CFOs are facing this reality every day. They're finding that the New Age doesn't mean that they are going to be replaced by AI; instead, they are being replaced by a New Age CFO who knows how to work side-by-side with AI, ML, and big data.

THE NEW AGE CFO

Most CFOs I know didn't envision working so closely with software developers and programmers, but this is the reality for the New Age CFO. The business world is moving really fast. If you got your CPA or your finance degree twenty years ago, you were probably working with different tools than what are available to you now. You were also building a skill set to capitalize on the tools you had available—and that skill set has changed, too. The New Age CFO knows how to adapt, use the tools in front of them, and develop a skill set that uses these tools to help their team as it undergoes a digital transformation.

I'm not saying that every CFO needs to go out and get a degree in computer science, but a New Age CFO needs to understand that their competitors understand coding and they should, too. I'm far from fluent in any coding language, but I've been able to educate myself enough that I understand what the developers, information technology team members, and programmers across the table are talking about. When CFOs don't understand these team members, they're only going to create problems for themselves. They're going to buy software that doesn't integrate well with what they have or they end up wasting big data and they don't even know it.

Business data falls under the finance department, which means that data falls under the New Age CFO. If you're going to be dealing with the data, you need to know how to access it. To know how to access the data you have available to you, you need to know a little bit about coding. It's integral to CFOs and anyone who's in a business position to work with data and software systems, even if you're not going to be programming them. The New Age CFO knows what is going on behind the curtain.

EXPANDING YOUR VALUE

Finance guys were never expected to peek behind the curtain, nor have they typically been engineers or developers. Historically, they have not questioned how the software tools they use work or how they talk to other systems in the company. The needs of modern business, however, are requiring CFOs to broaden their skill sets. They have to be the ones to make the right changes and put their company on a path to a digital transformation.

This feels like a big responsibility—almost one that is out of the typical CFO's depth. Think about how all the other groups look at finance. You've got operations, typically working the longest hours in the company. They have to get stuff done or else the entire company shuts down. Salespeople are in charge of bringing in new business. Marketing is working with sales to achieve their goals and ensure that the company grows. Historically, finance has been a department of bean counters in the background. After operations and sales and marketing have done their thing, we come into the meetings to tell everybody their score.

Old-school CFOs know that this can be tough on finance. Finance departments have typically been seen as a cost burden to the company. We report everything after the fact and don't add any real value to the company's bottom line. But the game has changed. If a finance department is automating the bean counting and moving their focus to sharing, interpreting, and using data, they can add real value to the company in real time.

Look at all the KPIs and metrics tracked by each department. You are already a key source of information. Start to think about what other information you could gather to make the data you have more valuable. Do you know how long it takes each customer to pay their invoices? Do you know how many times those customers call in with technical or service issues? Is there a correlation? Do customers who have to call in for support frequently take longer to pay their bills?

Who else in the company is going to ask questions like this? Expand your value and start thinking like a data scientist.

The modern CFO understands that the finance group can actually become a profit center for the company. You are the first to work with financial data. You are the person that the CEO, the board, other senior management, and employees down the line turn to for finance information. That information starts with financial reports, but finance also holds onto reports on what the company spends with each vendor, and how much revenue has come in by the individual customer, region, sales channel, etc. Knowledge is power, and by understanding how to use data and automate the most menial data-related tasks, you can gain more power and share that power with your team.

Invoicing clients, paying invoices, and doing reports aren't powerful job responsibilities—not when you compare them to taking all the data that you have, combining it with other data in the company, and becoming a strategic partner.

In the past decade, this has been a common transition in the CFO role, but only for CFOs who feel the need to grow and change within their position. If you want to move up in your current organization, or you want to take a job in a new organization, you have to speak the right language. You have to understand the New Age responsibilities of the New Age CFO. Senior leadership teams aren't looking for glorified bookkeepers who can pay and send invoices. You need to show where you bring value. And that value comes from the information and the depth.

THINK LIKE A CODER

This personal and professional transformation may sound more daunting than the digital transformation at your company, but it's okay if you've never stepped foot inside of a computer lab or written a line of code before. Your team knows that you aren't a software developer. Fortunately, the thought process for finance is not that different from the thought process of an engineer. You know the end goal and you know the steps you have to take to get there. It is just a matter of taking the steps to get from point A to point B.

With practice, coding becomes as easy to a developer as debits and credits are to an accountant. To the uninitiated, however, lines of code might as well be hieroglyphics for all the sense that can be made of them.

But you do not need to know how to code everything. Getting a basic understanding of coding enables you to think like a coder, which is enough. It will enable you to understand in broad strokes the functionality that is needed and be better able to explain it to the developer. Remember, you're not trying to switch careers; you're just trying to understand the landscape of the modern business world on a deeper level. To that end, if you are intimidated by a deep coding course, you can look for a more "broad strokes" type course that gives you the gist of the languages, tools, and concepts but doesn't get down into the nitty gritty.

Once you get the gist, you start to understand other concepts of programming: what a database actually is, how data comes out, and how that data sits in a raw form that's not easily digestible by humans. You will see how putting data in a web app gives you a much cleaner set of data to work with and share with your team. You're just trying to understand it enough so that it will help. It's a means to an end.

REDUCING CONFLICTS AND SOLVING PROBLEMS

In the early 2000s, before I was in finance, I was a product manager for a web design tool. This tool helped non-coders build their own websites (think WordPress before there was WordPress). We had a whole team of developers who worked on this tool along with a million other products and projects they supported. It turned out that marketing, where I worked, could dream up ideas about one hundred times faster than our development team could build them. As a result, the two groups stayed in a regular state of conflict.

When people who are requesting a project don't understand the level of effort the work they're asking for requires, there is going to be conflict. Many times, the marketing team thought they were making minor requests, failing to see the ripple effect that touched their relationship to the development team *and* the final product. They didn't see this ripple effect because they didn't think like a developer.

I didn't want to have this strained relationship with the developers. I made sure I was able to speak their language. Every time I made a request, I wanted to let them know that I at least had a concept of how much work I was asking them to do. With this small bit of empathy, I was able to talk to them directly without their being defensive.

At one point, I wanted a product enhancement that I knew wouldn't be a priority in the development cycle. I built it myself and then showed it to the developers. I wasn't a coder then as I'm not a coder now, but I managed to get 80 percent of the work done for them. All they had to do was clean it up and roll it into the product. This really pushed our relationship forward—I became a weird unicorn to them. I was a guy in marketing that could code and had actually built something myself. This relationship made it easier for me to get the product enhancements and developments that I wanted, and it opened my eyes to the importance of this mentality. If I wanted to work with developers, I had to think like a developer, even when I was in marketing.

This mentality has proven itself to be useful again and again in my career.

When I started in the retail business, we had point-of-sale systems that weren't talking to each other. It was difficult to track sales at multiple units when we couldn't consolidate the data into a single repository. The previous finance team knew what they wanted but could not effectively describe it. The software manufacturer was slow to innovate, and the company was at its mercy regarding what was available. When I came in, I stopped asking them to build something. Instead, I asked them for access to the data. Once access had been granted, we were able to build out an API that consolidated information from all units into a single database. That was my first step towards finance automation with this company.

Another sign of outdated processes I've looked at with each new company I've joined is overly complicated Excel spreadsheets used to perform routine tasks. Managing complex processes through spreadsheets always makes me nervous. One broken formula or fat-fingered cell can cause ripple effects that could break the whole system

In my most recent position, I inherited an overly complex Excel-based process for calculating sales commissions. The previous finance team used this massive spreadsheet that was updated from multiple sources on multiple tabs, and historical data had to be preserved month over month, so the spreadsheet just kept getting bigger and more unmanageable every time it was used. By the time I got there it took almost two minutes just to open this massive file. The commissions were calculated by one guy every month, and he was the only person in the company who knew how to do this. We used to joke that his system involved some pivot tables, VLOOKUPs, a handful of chicken bones, and a star chart!

Excel is, of course, every finance guy's favorite tool. We love to brag about all the cool things we can do in it. But at times, we become the handyman who only has one tool in his toolbox. Just as a handyman can't fix every problem with a hammer, a finance guy can't fix every problem with a spreadsheet.

My solution to the giant Excel problem was to dump all the historical data into a MySQL database I built on my laptop and to write queries to pull the new data from the appropriate systems each month. I'm *really* slow at writing SQL queries, but even then I knew that if I could power through and make this query work, I could save myself (or whoever else was going to have to calculate commissions going forward) hours upon hours every month going forward.

After many, many hours of SQL hacks, I finally produced a series of workable queries that could pull all of the data required for the report. Each of these queries could be run in under five minutes, and suddenly my team had several days of free time which could now be spent on more productive tasks each month!

This took place at a small company—the leadership team did not have to make any additional hires or even dip into their budget to solve this problem and save themselves five days a week each month. You can do this at your company no matter how big it is. All you have to do is learn the language of the developers on your team and have a curious mind for how this works.

How to Learn These Skills

If you've stuck with me this long, you probably have a curious mind and a desire to upgrade to the position of New Age CFO.

You don't have to get another master's degree in order to speak the language of developers. The right path for you depends on where you are in your career, what your company can offer, and how much time you have available to gain this knowledge. Ideally, you would want to be on a cross-departmental team with developers and have a mentorship where you and a developer teach each other the basics of your field. But that's not possible or practical on many teams. Most people will have to take a class, whether that is at a local university or online with a self-paced course. You don't *have* to break the bank to earn university credits—a basic coding class with Udemy or Coursera can give you a certificate for fifty dollars. The knowledge is even out there for free, you just have to be willing to go out on a limb and try something new.

You may find that as soon as you dip a toe into analytics or data science, you start to feel the call to move beyond the comfortable world of Excel. You might start using Tableau and learning more about what you can do with data visualization. As you continue to experiment, you might find yourself wanting to marry two databases—then you'll go down a rabbit hole of query languages and coding.

If your motivation is to be a data-driven company or department or individual in the company, you will find a way to get there. You've just got to be willing to put in the work and push those doors open when you arrive in front of them.

Management By Walking Around

You already know how much you as a CFO can benefit from learning this new skill set. Your business will improve, too. But as we continue to talk about the financial automation team, it's important to remember that you are not doing this alone.

If you're going to put an automation plan in place, you need to thoroughly understand it to the point where you can communicate it to others. At each step of the process, you have to be able to explain to the CEO and the CIO what you're trying to do. If you can't speak intelligently, distinctly, and thoroughly about the plan, then you're not likely to get the buy-in you need. If you leave it to another senior leader, you may not end up with the product you want. Unfortunately, all the heavy lifting, architecting, cheerleading, and training fall on your shoulders. But this heavy lifting is worth it when all of the grunt work is finally removed in your digital transformation.

Assuming all the people in leadership across the company are intelligent, curious, and interested in improving the company, you don't need to turn them into experts of finance automation, either. You just need to get them to understand the importance of your mission and get them to buy-in to the process.

Thinking beyond the C-suite, you will also need to understand everyone's processes and speak their language in order to complete an audit at the beginning of your digital transformation. At my current company, I didn't have this opportunity and it ended up slowing down my process. The company hired people in multiple states across the country, so I couldn't visit everyone and talk to them about their processes. I would have much preferred to go sit with everyone, talk to them about what they were doing, look over their shoulder for a day or two, and review any documentation that was related to their processes. But instead, because I wasn't able to do that, I had to do a more formal audit. No one wants to be audited. People were defensive throughout the process and took a long time to give me the feedback and information I needed. If I had been able to see them individually, speak their language, and share my intentions for our transformation, I would have had a much easier time getting everyone on board.

This process requires you to know how to assign people based on their strengths and abilities. If someone is not a great communicator, they have to be paired with someone else on the team who is. Just as with any project, you have to know your team's strengths, weaknesses, opportunities, and threats in order to manage accordingly.

The best way to do this is to "manage by walking around."

This is a term often associated with Jack Welch, the former CEO of General Electric. The idea behind managing by walking around is that the leader walks around, talks to everybody, and gets everyone out of their desks to interact with each other. It's hard to tell a bunch of finance guys and programmers to get away from their desks, but sitting behind that desk isn't a natural work environment. Sitting together, without a big metal desk in front of you, makes both parties more approachable.

This can be critical in understanding what needs to be done before a digital transformation, even if you are not the CEO of the company. If you get up from your desk and spend time talking to the front-line employees and managers, you can get a better grasp of what they are doing and what their needs will be during the transformation. When the finance guy walks down to the warehouse to see what everyone is doing, they will see people in their work environment.

This is a very informal management style with the goal of getting to know the employees and the problems of the company. Ultimately, you need to understand what they're doing; you have to get their support to help you streamline the process. While you have these conversations, you can share your knowledge with them, too.

The New Age CFO speaks the language of everyone in the company because they are working with everyone in the company to complete this digital transformation. They let their curiosity take them beyond number crunching and bean counting into the worlds of RStudio, SQL, and Tableau. They have such a grasp on understanding automation and AI that they can educate and "sell" these concepts to anyone. This is important because it's necessary—everyone must be on board for these processes to transform your company.

II.

The New Age CFO is leading the charge when it comes to finance automation, but in reality, these changes reach across all departments in the company. They can't happen in a vacuum—it is part of an overall digital transformation that requires cross-functional support from all groups within the organization.

It requires the right technologies, the right systems, and the right support from all departments. That support starts with senior leadership.

Let's go through the key players in the finance automation team who support the CFO through the overall digital transformation.

Chief Executive Officer (CEO)

The CEO is the head honcho, the big cheese. Without her support, your plan won't get very far. This is why you need to learn the language of developers and have an understanding of what finance automation entails. Learn your needs and requirements, understand what it will take to get your automation plan in place, and go knock her socks off with the brilliance of your plan and your detailed roadmap for how to get there.

The old-school thinking of how the CEO goes about decision making as it relates to data must be replaced before a digital transformation occurs. Without data, the CEO would have a hunch and go off on that hunch alone. But now, the game has changed. The CEO might have a hunch, but then you can look at the data to turn that hunch into a hypothesis. The availability of this data becomes another advisory point for you. Instead of just listening to opinions, the CEO has hard facts behind their decisions. A digital transformation is extremely valuable to their position—and you must learn how to communicate that to them.

Chief Information Officer (CIO)

The CIO is responsible for overseeing the company's IT infrastructure. Her focus is typically on improving operational efficiency by ensuring systems are always online and available. She will work to make them as reliable and efficient as possible.

There are two avenues successful companies traverse simultaneously: explore and exploit. Explore requires you to look at new opportunities. Exploit requires you to do what you do as well as possible. The CIO is focused on exploiting the existing network. The leader of finance automation is about exploring new opportunities.

Just as CFOs don't typically know software, CIOs don't typically know finance. But because you are looking to change the very nature of your department, the onus is on you to learn enough to speak to the CIO and get her on your side.

You might not have a CIO at your company—not a lot of small businesses do. But if you do, bring them on your journey to becoming the New Age CFO. If you're having a hard time learning the language of your developers, the CIO can be a translator for you.

Chances are, if your company has filled this position, you're probably further along in the digital transformation process. If your company hasn't, you might need to become the CFO, CIO, and Chief Data Officer (CDO) all at once. This is where you're going to increase your value to the organization. By grabbing this data and information and owning it like the CIO and the CDO do, you become a strategic partner and elevate the whole department.

Chief Operations Officer (COO)

The operations guy has a lot on his plate. He's scrambling around making sure the warehouse is adequately staffed, inventory levels are correct, and watching production levels like a hawk.

He could lead the automation project, sure. This guy could lead a parade of cats through a field of prairie dogs without skipping a beat. But like the CIO, the COO is all about exploiting the existing system. It's highly unlikely that he's going to be able to step out of the "now" to plan automation for the finance department. And it's almost unfortunate that the COO is likely too busy to take this on; operations guys love this kind of planning. This is the world that operations guys live in. Plus, their processes and position are probably more defined than anyone else's. COOs appreciate real-time information, probably more than anyone. If they can see our production efficiency is off by 20 percent on a certain day, they'll start planning a solution immediately. They thrive when they need to act quickly. Having data in real time makes their life significantly easier, and they're going to really benefit from predictive analytics. They're on your side, even when you can't reach them immediately.

Chief Data Officer (CDO)

Some New Age companies have a CDO. If you have a CDO, then you might have a harder time, or be completely restricted from leading the charge on finance automation. You don't automatically have to be the sole authority to be the master of this data—the CDO serves as the authority and the hero. But most likely, you don't have a CDO, so you've got to lead the charge.

GET EVERYONE TOGETHER TO AGREE

Identifying the players isn't enough—you must facilitate the conversations. You have to sit down with the rest of the management team and agree upon what processes you are going to retain and what needs to be automated. Everyone has to gather together the platforms their team uses, identify the most accurate systems, and consolidate the data.

Get everyone to nod their heads and say "yes" throughout every step of this communication. If everybody's in agreement on where the data comes from and what you're using as the data, then you can avoid any party becoming accusatory. Everyone is looking at the data the same way despite their very different roles in the company. No one is spending any time arguing over the nuances of the vocabulary and systems that you use. Then, you're focused more on why certain problems occurred and what solutions will help you all move forward.

When data is democratized, no one can hide. Everyone is held accountable.

III.

To make finance automation a reality, you need to assemble a team of managers, developers, and data scientists. Each of these team players will have specific roles and responsibilities that will be outlined shortly. You don't want to micromanage every aspect of the project. You want to architect it from on high and have it be led by people who understand the task before them and are empowered to make it happen.

Once again, it's important to speak the language of what you want and what each team player will be doing in their new role. People hate change. The people on the implementation team have to be excellent communicators and it has to start with you. Everyone has to be able to explain to everyone in the company how this change will benefit them. They have to be personable, intelligent, and willing to dig in and get their hands dirty while coaching others through the process. They need to know finance and have a foundational understanding of processes across the company, but they also have to understand software and data in general, so they see how information flows through the process, where it resides, and how to get to it.

Keep these traits in mind as you build your team. If you have the perfect budget or a big company set up, you can give individuals each of these roles. I will warn you—I've never been at a company where you have all the people that fill these roles. You will most likely have to wear several hats. And in the worst-case scenario, you're wearing all the hats.

But what hats need to be worn? Let's look at the six main roles.

AUTOMATION LEAD

The automation lead is a jack-of-all-trades, but a project leader first and foremost. The individual has good soft skills and previous experience at your company as a communicator, a manager, and a problem solver. They already know how the processes work. What is most important is that the lead has a blend of finance and technical skills and can translate across departments.

If your company is big enough, this position isn't you. This position is the field sergeant, and you are the general orchestrating the entire project from headquarters. In a small company, or with a limited budget, you'll wear both hats.

CHANGE AGENT

The change agent has a similar skill set to an automation lead, however they're typically higher up in the management structure. This person has to get buy-in from many people who probably aren't happy about making changes. A change agent is the cheerleader for the whole automation project. He understands the people, processes, and culture across groups in your company. He can communicate up and down the chain of command like a salesperson with the ability to pitch the final picture and explain to all departments that their lives are going to be better, and everyone is going to be doing more meaningful work.

This person also has to be able to adapt to ongoing changes and unexpected hurdles. The change agent is fast on his feet and able to adjust course on the fly.

If you have an automation lead and a change agent, you are on Easy Street. You still have an entire transformation to undergo, but you are definitely a step ahead of those who don't have these team members and have to wear these hats themselves.

Technical Architect

The technical architect is responsible for designing the entire software system required to make this automation initiative possible. This is the person you will work with to translate your overall integration plan into a symphony of computer code that makes the whole system work together.

They're highly technical people. They're code-savvy and they can speak the language of developers. But they're not just any old developers—they have moved up the ranks and can be the architect to the developer's carpenter. They set priorities for the coders using an Agile mindset. If you have a change agent and an automation lead, they're defining the scope of all these projects with a technical architect.

If you find yourself in a position where you are serving as the chief financial officer, the automation lead, the change agent, and the technical architect, good luck. The likelihood of finding a single person who can serve all these roles is about as rare as finding an Inverted Jenny. And the rare person who can serve all of these roles will probably cost just as much.

CODERS

These hackers are the experts that are building the tools that you look for, and they'll be your best friends if you treat them right. Bring them doughnuts. Watch *The Expanse* series and read the books. Catch them at the water cooler and explain to them why the series is actually better than the books. Order them pizzas. But don't bother them when they're working. Let them know you love them from afar.

In an Agile world, this is your core team. But they're not going to be able to do anything until you know what you want and can communicate it to the technical architect. The technical architect will gather the coders around, tell them your story, and together they'll figure out what it will take to bring the story to life. Chances are, no matter how good you might be as a coder, if you're not coding, they probably don't want you looking over their shoulders and telling them how to write their SQL queries or whatever lines of code they are working on. That's why the technical architect is so crucial to this team—they act as a liaison so you're not bothering anyone.

Finance Lead

This gal may not be able to code her way out of a paper bag, but she knows finance as well as anyone in the department. She knows every process and procedure across the finance organization and can explain them well enough to the technical team that they will be able to interpret her process descriptions into code.

The coders and the finance leader are probably never talking to each other directly. They're going through the change agent, the technical architect, and the automation lead. But the coder and the finance leader are experts in their specific field.

Again, if you're in a small organization, you may take on the role of the finance lead *and* have to understand the basics of coding. But if you can delegate these tasks to someone who is an expert in finance, you can take this hat off and fill whatever gaps are missing on your team.

Data Scientists

We've touched on data scientists and how hard it is to find one. You may get one. You may get a team of them. These are the people who help you gather and analyze the data to figure out the reports you need.

They understand enough of the coding to be dangerous, but they also understand different areas of business. Part of being a data scientist is you have to speak the language of developers and then speak the language of the customers. By "customers," I mean the people who work and benefit from the automation and from the data that you're providing them. Their job includes interpreting the sales pipeline to forecast sales or looking at the financial pipeline to build a budget. For years, this has been the fastest growing and highest-paid position in the business world.

Everybody wants data scientists. They're in such high demand and hard to find. Most likely, you will have to rely on upscaling your existing employees to do this job. It is not a fast process. You've got to have an eye for people who have the willingness and propensity to learn this stuff. You've got to set the expectation early on; you've got to encourage them. Then it takes a long time—it's hard to know when you're ready to start implementing automation. You've got to get the team structured how you want; you've got to have a base level of confidence that your team is going to be able to do what you want.

This team cannot be built overnight, but keeping an eye out for the right employees to upscale and the right hires to make will ensure that this team works together, speaks the "right" languages, and knows how to work within your existing team to encourage and sell a digital transformation.

HIRING AND TRAINING

The best way to build this team varies so much by the type of company you're in and what you have available. I will offer one piece of universal advice: you want this team to be cross-departmental. You can't just tell the finance team to figure out automation for everyone. Operations and sales aren't going to get on board when the only people talking about a project are the boring finance people. You need to find champions in each department that are interested in automation and can communicate this enthusiasm back to their team, build momentum, and change the mindset of the company.

Some leaders may prefer to hire outside data scientists or leaders who have specialties not currently present in their company. How does that leader find a great team of data scientists? This can be very difficult, and I'd typically recommend that a hiring manager get help when hiring for a skilled position outside of their own expertise. If you're hiring a developer, I'd look to someone in IT or research and development within your organization to vet their technical skills before you can evaluate them on their understanding of your mission.

I learned this the hard way. A few years ago I worked for a streaming audio company when I received a recommendation for a data scientist. The candidate came in to interview and he said all the right stuff during an hour interview—he could talk the talk. The marketing guy agreed with me after his hour-long interview. The candidate made it to the final step of the interview, where he spoke to the CTO. It only took the CTO thirty minutes to recognize that the candidate could only talk the talk, not walk the walk. We would have hired the guy if it weren't for the CTO, and the candidate would have been a disaster. You have to rely on a hiring manager or someone from the technical side of the company to do the final parts of the interview and make decisions on who to hire.

Throughout my career, I've also had a training budget for my department. Because I've been focused on finance automation for so long, I have a pretty clear path I like to encourage my employees to follow to get them where I want them. The path has been different for each person, but it typically starts with getting them to become experts in the existing software systems we use. I had my current admin take every class available on our accounting system and payroll system. Then I had her sign up for Excel courses. I told her that she may not have come into the job wanting to be a finance person, but by the time she left, she would be. In this case, I haven't gotten her into any data science training yet, but she is the lead on getting stuff done within our software systems. I think it's important to push employees in a direction, but if that's not their interest, you're not going to make them happier by making them train on something that is ultimately outside of their career or personal interest and comfort zone.

Upskilling shouldn't stop once you have assigned the roles of data scientist or technical architect. Critical thinking and data literacy are important at every level in the organization. I always encourage my bookkeeper to take more accounting courses. I want my managers to take more advanced training in project management and other specialties. When I am working with a company, employees are constantly training as individuals and within their own teams. To establish a data-driven culture, hire for upskilling and help existing employees transform. With enough buy-in from the top, you could make data and analytics training required in the company. (This is easier said than done, but wouldn't it be nice?)

Everyone Is Involved

A data-driven culture requires that everyone be aware of the importance of automation rather than just leaving it to the CEO or management team to make decisions. Every department needs to buy-in to the idea of using ERP systems and automation to make their lives easier and the company more efficient. Once everyone has bought in and everyone is in agreement about how data is going to be used, you will have a much easier time managing your teams and reaching the larger goals of financial automation. This will require getting everyone on board and shifting culture, but the effort put into these changes will pay off in the long run. As a New Age CFO, you believe this to be true—now your financial automation team needs to believe it.

PART 6.

How to Bring Management and Team Members on Board

I.

Hiring the right team and setting up training are just the beginning steps of a much larger goal: creating a data culture that is required for finance automation. Because your company will be a leader in this type of culture, you have to be intentional about how you bring management and team members on board. You must build and foster trust, share your knowledge, and follow through on your commitment to automation and data. This commitment starts at the top of the company or department, and it starts with good communication.

Throughout this book, you have learned the benefits of finance automation and data. You have spent a lot of time thinking about how these ideas apply to your company. Now you have to share them with everyone. Get everyone buzzing about this transformation before you even make your official pitch. Do not worry if you don't have the resources available to undergo a full transformation immediately or even if you aren't the CFO. You have options for getting everyone on board, both through pitching and planning appropriately.

WHAT'S YOUR PITCH?

Finance automation should not be considered an optional cost, but a required update to your company's entire back-office process. You may not have to spend the money this year or even next, but in the long run, the change is inevitable and required for successful enterprises in the future. Moving from analog to digital processes is key to business success.

There are many ways to approach "pitching" this mindset to your team members. You could help them look at the benefits of automation from a practical standpoint. You could calculate the ROI of automation. You might choose to make small changes, and once the results of these changes are in, share the results to ask for the next step. The right approach depends on your team and what resources you have available to you.

THE PRACTICAL PITCH

When I came to my current company, I observed that all the salespeople would submit their expense reports through an Excel template. The CFO before me made the template; every month, every salesperson would start with a blank template and fill it in. Inevitably, I think every salesperson in the company, every month, broke that template. The auto sum wouldn't work, the sales tax would disappear, and the formulas would completely warp the final numbers. Nobody was breaking this template maliciously—they just weren't Excel people.

I envisioned something different. What if I gave them an online form that they couldn't break? They couldn't manipulate the data and we could collect the data with more trust in whatever numbers were coming in.

As technology advanced, I was able to think in more efficient ways to make this vision a reality. Now, you can purchase off-the-shelf software that scans a receipt just by taking a picture of it. The software can identify what type of expense it is—gas, travel, dining, etc. It smartly goes ahead and codes everything. This way is much more efficient than broken Excel templates no one knew how to use in the first place.

The benefits of implementing this software affected everyone, from the salesperson who didn't know how to use Excel to the CFO who built the spreadsheet. These are the stories that have to be shared in order to get team members on board and establish a data-driven culture.

This practical element can be necessary because getting everyone on board is not just about how much automation is going to cost or about how much you're going to get out of it. People are thinking about their everyday lives when they make these decisions, even if they don't know what tasks they will have on their to-do list after automation is in place. When computers first came around, people weren't using computers in their business. It was a disruptive technology, just like the printing press was back in the 1400s and like financial automation is today. Think about all the new disruptive technologies that have been developed; there are always businesses that ride the front of the wave and get to pat themselves on the back because they implement more efficient technology before their competitors.

Your business still has a chance to be at the front of the wave, but if you're not acting in the next year or two, you're going to be left behind. You're going to be an out-of-date firm that doesn't have a full handle on the practical expectations of your customers or how easy and quick payment processes can be. The tools are out there, and more tools are being developed every day. It's a growing pain to adapt to them, but if you don't, it's going to be at your own peril. It may not be today, it may not be tomorrow, but it is going to be in the next five to ten years. You're going to be significantly behind your competitors, regardless of your industry.

WHAT'S THE ROI?

Cutting-edge companies are already experimenting with advanced analytics. The availability of data and new skills that capitalize on that data through analytics are providing value to organizations. While it may be difficult to put an exact dollar value on this type of information, data-driven companies are capitalizing on data to make better decisions across the board.

When you start to make moves to automate, you might find that the costs aren't as high as you imagined. Take inventory of your existing processes and evaluate the level of manual effort versus automation. Look at the potential value of automation and the level of feasibility of automating. How complex are they? What will be required to automate? In this phase, you don't need to figure out "how," you just need to know what systems need to communicate in order to pull it off. Engage business unit leaders to help evaluate. Review existing technologies and systems and what is lacking. Again, the solutions themselves do not have to be set in stone. All you need to do is show your team that the pain points that plague them now will be a thing of the past when more processes are automated.

Because the automation project will have impacts across the company, it may be easier to think of ROI for each area you impact.

If you're automating the expense reporting process, for example, how much time did it previously take to collect and process expense reports? How long did it take to reimburse employees? How common were errors in the expense reporting process?

If the change in expense reporting results in two hours less of work for the accounts payable clerk, factor in her hourly rate. Were expense reports frequently delayed due to the time it took to process? Can you put a value on the elimination of delayed payments? Maybe it adds to the greater happiness of employees who don't have to wait for expense reimbursements.

At first glance, these are small changes. But there will be bigger projects and bigger successes. What if you can fully automate your invoice process? Does that eliminate the need for one or more accounts receivable clerks? How much time is saved by freeing up the team that used to put together invoices? We've given numerous examples in this book, and you will have many of your own, but once you start looking at automation as a series of projects, you will be able to start finding cost savings across the board.

STARTING SMALL

When you don't have another choice, you can pick off low-hanging fruit and show your team how sweet automation can taste. That is what I did at my company now. Plenty of off-the-shelf software comes with a monthly charge that isn't going to be a capital investment. By "low-hanging fruit," I mean expense tracking, procurement, or paying bills. The software that automates these processes are web-based with mobile phone apps or applications that you can get that can hook into any accounting system.

Find one of these off-the-shelf inexpensive products that do something like handle expenses. Previously, your team might have handled expenses by filling out a spreadsheet. One person writes, "On October 3rd, I went to Boise, Idaho, and I drove three hundred miles." The other person writes, "$40 gas conference 6/22/2021." You already know how frustrating this can be for everyone on the accounting team. An off-the-shelf product, like the one I mentioned earlier, only requires that the team member takes a photo of their receipt. Everything is automated and reimbursed properly—no one must spend half a day each month going through expense reports and cleaning up everything.

If you've got a forward-looking, senior management team that is doing this on the front of the house already, then you don't need to start small. They'll hear the pitch of your grand vision and approve your automation strategy. But if the whole company is on the wrong side of the digital transformation wave, it makes more sense to take this approach and do something small. Take baby steps and walk them through small victories. This isn't a bad approach if it's what gets your team members on board. When employees and managers see the impact of automation and increased data, the approach to business problems will change. Automation increases available data and frees up employee time. Everyone is more empowered to research and make recommendations.

Starting small tackles one of the biggest challenges of pitching finance automation to your team. It's one thing to assist your team in envisioning the intangibles that you have to sell and believing in the value automation will bring across the organization. It's another thing to go through a small transformation and say, "Look, our competitors are doing this and more, which means they're going to be more efficient and more streamlined. They took the gamble on a larger change. Will you?"

WHO DO YOU TALK TO?

I think being a great communicator is as important as any of the skills that have been discussed in this book. If you're lucky enough to have a platform where you can address the company all at once, you can talk about this beautiful (and sometimes painful) journey that you're going to take them on through digital transformation. You can map out the beautiful and efficient destination you will all reach together.

CFOs usually have access to this type of platform over an analyst, or procurement manager. But even in these junior positions, you can get the ball rolling on a digital transformation. You have to get permission to talk to the right people or inject yourself into cross-departmental meetings. When I was a more junior employee starting out on this road, I'd have to ask my boss for permission to build the finance automation team and ask for resources from other departments. I didn't have the decision-making ability and authority to move forward as easily as I do in a CFO position. It was only when the CFO got comfortable with my ideas that we started to access and use data from sales and finance in the ways that I had envisioned.

You're ready to roll the dice! You know the benefits of automation and the future of finance by reading this book and being an expert in your field. Who is going to join you at the table?

II.

It's your turn to bring management and your team members on board with finance automation. These are the steps to take to establish and sell your plan to automate the finance function within your organization and lead your organization into the digital world.

It's time to move out of the theoretical and into the new reality. Don't just read through this section —make notes and use it as a checklist to mark your progress. You will find the guides to each of these steps throughout the book. Not all of these steps can be completed overnight. Copy and laminate the information below and keep it in your desk drawer. When you reach the end of these steps, pick up the book again and reread the section on building your team. You will be well on your way to setting up a stellar group of people who will, harkening back to the earlier metaphor, "eat the elephant one bite at a time."

CHECKLIST

DEFINE FINANCE TRANSFORMATION

Finance transformation involves the expansion of the finance department into a strategic, forward-looking organization that becomes the central figure in an organization's strategic initiatives by integrating new technology (APIs, databases, and data science) to provide greater management insights. CFOs can become key members of the strategic leadership team. Finance becomes fast, efficient, accurate. By defining the transformation ahead, you can give senior leaders and your entire team a peek into the future.

GET CROSS-FUNCTIONAL BUY-IN

You must have the support and buy-in of the entire senior leadership team. They must understand your automation mission. This book has shown you the general steps you must take. You need to apply them to your organization and map out your plan.

If needed, create a steering committee from the different departments which will engage key leaders in the company. Seek their contributions and help bring them on board with your vision.

Set goals and have the team help you create a roadmap on how you will get there. Before you can calculate an ROI for your project, you need to take a few steps to understand where you are and where you're going. These questions will help clarify your journey:

- What is the end goal with your finance automation plan? Why are you doing it?
- Choose metrics that match the "why" of the automation plan.
- Start with where you are today:
- What are your current expenses?
- What are your current staffing needs?
- Where will you be when the project is complete?
- How will you measure cost savings?
- Will there be operational efficiencies (e.g., headcount reductions or software system eliminations)?
- Are there revenue impacts—not just cost savings?
- Does automation reduce customer churn? Are there tasks that are made easier through improved invoicing and customer data tracking that help keep customers happy and reduce churn?

- Does automation increase your business value to customers?
- What is the cost of the automation project in terms of headcount required and software development? (These costs are real whether you buy or build your software).

Work through these questions one by one before you prepare your pitch. This will not only help you strengthen the definition of your finance transformation, but also engage people throughout all departments who may respond differently to different pitches.

IDENTIFY ROADBLOCKS

You can't ignore roadblocks—the most cynical team members will be waiting for them to pop up and disrupt your vision for the company. Identify them ahead of time and plan for ways through them.

Ask yourself the following questions:

- What are the skills of your existing employees?
- Can employees be trained to learn new skills, or is a new group of employees required for this new transition?
- Are current processes so inefficient and misaligned that you're still not clear how to streamline them?

Work through these questions by gathering information and pain points. Understanding the bumps in the road will be crucial to your success.

BUILD YOUR TRAVEL PLAN

What goals and deliverables are at the heart of your finance automation project? Document and communicate these. Then, ask yourself how you will get there. Can you do it with existing staff, or do you have to bring in outside help? Who will fill what role, and when do you need to put on multiple hats? Prepare for the role you will play on the journey.

DEFINE METRICS

How will you measure your success?

This process begins with looking at the gaps between your current state and desired end state. I'm not just speaking about the practical, everyday tasks of your finance team. What gaps hold your company back from having a data-driven culture? When everything is said and done, how will your team members approach and use data? Identify how you can bridge those gaps. What does "The Promised Land" of finance automation look like at your company?

PREPARE YOUR PITCH

You've identified the problems and hashed out a plan with department heads across the organization. Now it's time to take your plan to the CEO and board. Build a business case and present it to leadership. Focus on both quantitative and qualitative aspects of your plan. Look at costs versus benefits and spell out the desired end state.

You can use any of the pitch styles that were outlined in this chapter, or a combination of multiple styles. What matters is that you have thought through the transformation you want to make, the plan for avoiding inevitable roadblocks, and you know the metrics you are using to measure your success.

Build Your Team and Engage Other Departments

If all goes well, it's time to implement the plan! Whether you are starting slow with one piece of software or undergoing a full transformation, your first step is building your team and getting everyone involved. Refer back to the previous chapter when you have reached this stage to refresh yourself on how to build your team.

FINAL THOUGHTS: WELCOME TO THE PROMISED LAND

Original image used by author's permission (Hayes Roberts)

One day, a New Age CFO will arrive at his desk, put down his jetpack, and ask his robot assistant to bring him his favorite cup of coffee. His computer will respond with a snarky comment before opening up a dashboard with constantly moving statistics regarding his company's financials, security footage of his flying car in the parking garage, and the option to bring the people in his video conference to life through a hologram.

Okay, we're not there *yet*. Maybe by the time I publish a second book, we can talk about robot assistants that also make coffee!

Here's what the New Age CFO is actually doing in her fully automated finance organization in 2021: she walks into her office, grabs a cup of coffee from her Nespresso coffee machine, takes it to her desk, and logs into her computer through a thumbprint.

On the screen is a dashboard of company metrics. She sees that invoices went out on time and some customers have already paid: 1,257 invoices were sent, 31 were paid, and 1,226 are still open. There are also now 116 invoices that are 30 days past due. She clicks a button on the screen which asks her if she is sure she wants to send a reminder to those customers. She clicks "yes," and the reminders go out. Each reminder is personalized to its recipient. Some are sent out via email, some via text, and some are automated phone calls.

Next, our New Age CFO looks at accounts payable. She clicks on a list of checks ready to be processed, paying some and waiting on others. When she looks at the sales pipeline and revenue, she is able to project this month's revenue, based on historical data weighed against the current pipeline, with just one click. Another click brings up expenses, and she sees that there are no abnormalities compared to prior periods.

She sits back, sips her coffee, and opens up the *Wall Street Journal* online.

In the financial section, she reads a news story about the leading indicators of financial slowdown. Companies are paying their bills slower. She asks her computer, "What is the status of our aging receivables compared to this month last year?"

The computer reports back audibly, "Average days receivable this month is 47 compared to 43 last year and a three-year average of 44." She thinks again about the invoice reminders she just sent out. Is there something more she should do? Her computer chirps again: "Reminder, you have a 9:00 appointment with Danielle, who is interviewing for the new data scientist position."

"Show me Danielle's resume."

The resume comes up on the screen and the CFO looks at the candidate's credentials. She was a product manager at a large company, with an undergraduate degree in business and a master's degree in data science. Although she hasn't worked in finance before, she understands data.

This is the exact skill set our CFO needs.

Our CFO has linked all of her systems and has a full end-to-end view of the company's operations from sales prospect to sold to service delivery to invoicing and client management. She has access to all kinds of data on customer service calls, timeliness of bill payments, and service uptime. The current system is pretty good at FP&A, but she's still not doing everything that she can with the data and automation available to her.

After the success of her automation project, she is in the good graces of the CEO, who is amazed at the amount of accessible data that is not being used. With some more data science, the CFO reassures the CEO, they can take their digital transformation to the next level. Improved data analysis management can elevate the company's ability to make decisions and be productive while saving money on compliance and marketing.

When it comes time to interview Danielle, the CFO finishes her coffee and goes out to greet her. She decides to do the interview while walking around. While physically walking around the office, the two metaphorically walk through the phases of the business, starting with sales. Our New Age CFO greets the outside sales manager, who is looking at a report of customers who have filled out questionnaires from the company's website.

The data scientist asks what they're doing with the data: "What's the conversion rate for customers who fill out a questionnaire?" The sales manager shares the answer, but the data scientist pushes further. "What do the customers who signed up have in common?" She wants to know more about the customers—not just whether they signed up or not.

The CFO is impressed with her inquisitive mind and the way she pursues answers. Their next stop is walking from sales to service delivery. They talk about how long it takes to get customers installed and how that timeline has been trending in recent months. Danielle asks where the bottlenecks are. They look at each point and identify them.

After service delivery, they go to customer care. They talk about call metrics and the number of customer complaints each month; they also discuss customer satisfaction and churn. The CFO continues to be impressed with the candidate and they walk back to her office for a more formal sit-down interview.

Danielle says she is impressed with how much data the company has on its entire process, but is confused about why she is interviewing with the CFO. "I'm not a finance person," she says. The CFO knows that and she explains the transformation her company has undergone in recent months and how it made sense for that project to fall under the finance department.

They talk about how the next step in transformation is more incremental. The previous steps of the digital transformation have allowed them to collect the required data, but they have to get better at using it.

The scenario I have shared is not the result of a *complete* digital transformation, although it might sound light-years away from what most CFOs are doing right now. This is the reality that you and your finance team could be living thanks to automation and data. And it starts with leadership seeing this Promised Land and promising these results to their CEO.

How Long Until We Reach the Promised Land?

A lot of companies won't go near the idea of a digital transformation because it's such a transformative shift from the way they do business and the way finance has been done for decades. Digital transformation is not an overnight process, but one that you have become familiar with while reading this book. How many other finance guys or operations guys who aren't in the business of ML know what it is? You may not have even begun to assess your company's processes or reached out to build a team of data scientists. That's okay. By bringing yourself up to speed, you are still riding the front of the wave of digital transformation that most companies don't even see on the horizon.

You don't have to ride this wave alone. If you really pull off this automation, you're doing it not just for you, but for everyone in the company. Everyone's roles become elevated through automation and digital transformation—you all reach your own version of the Promised Land together. But if you don't have unlimited resources, and you don't have a team with the necessary skill sets, or you don't have a team at all, the digital transformation is only going to take longer. You have to get everybody on board. Pass this book off to your CEO, COO, or other leaders on your team. They might learn a thing or two about ML and AI, too.

If you or others on your senior leadership team don't know what you can do with the data to help drive product development, to help interpret and anticipate customer needs, or to elevate human resources, you have a lot more learning to do. Anyone coming into the business world now can ride this wave. Nobody's saying you're going to have to sit in front of a blinking cursor and do the coding, but everything you and your team do can run through some kind of computer system and directly impact your bottom line.

If you want to get stuff done and move this transformation along, your team has to be able to speak your developers' language and understand what they are doing. If you don't know anything about the field, then you won't know how to anticipate how long it will take for deliverables and what requests are reasonable. Whether you're building the products within your digital transformation or not, you can at least speak the language. That's going to make it much more efficient for you to get this automation done. You may not know the language today, but at least you know that this is the next step on your journey. So take that next step and move closer to the Promised Land.

EPILOGUE

The below was originally a featured essay for the 2021 Harvard Beacon Business Analytics Conference. I wanted to include it here as a reminder that while all the modern technology out there now greatly empowers leaders to make better decisions, it is important we treat this new technology as a tool—an aid—to decision making, and not an autonomous decision maker meant to replace human judgment.

Unbounded Rationality

THE FUTURE OF DECISION MAKING IN AN AI-DRIVEN WORLD

All of the great endeavors in human history started with a decision. From early voyages across vast and unknown oceans to the discovery of the double helix structure of DNA, our choices have defined not only the world in which we live, but our humanity itself.

For leaders, bringing a vision to fruition requires myriad decisions—big and small—about people, projects, and principles intertwining to create a holistic outcome. Great leaders rise above baser instincts, emotional responses, and distractions. They draw upon all of the skills, tools, and counsel at their disposal. This is how great decisions are made.

WELCOME TO THE MACHINE

While presidents have cabinets, CEOs have boards, and Macbeth consulted witches, modern leaders are increasingly incorporating data and analytics to guide decisions. With the help of data science, they are able to better discern signals from a vast ocean of noise.

However, to lead effectively in the Age of AI, managers must be able to understand and trust the source of that signal, lest they be fooled by a digital Fata Morgana. Magellan sailed around the world using data from sextants and compasses, but it was the human drive for discovery that propelled that voyage forward. Conversely, Macbeth made tragic choices based on his "strange intelligence." Whether the source be witches or robots, leaders must be able to discern the nature and validity of the data they are provided.

There is a tendency to believe AI-driven algorithms are more rational than humans, but math is inherently no more rational than a toaster. If leaders are to use algorithms, they must understand the data upon which their decisions are based and the logic on which they were built, just as they would with data from any source—including their human advisors. For if they be Macbeth's "instruments of darkness that tell us truths," we must know this strange intelligence to which we owe.

Leaders don't need a PhD in mathematics to use AI any more than they require a doctorate in psychology to work with their human counterparts. Yet, a general understanding of each goes a long way to maximizing both. From back propagation to rumination, effective leaders must draw upon the totality of the tools available to them, yet cede authority to none. Like any great technological advancement, AI brings great promise but also great responsibility.

Algorithms will continue to improve and become increasingly valuable. But just as we would not completely surrender our shopping decisions to a website's product recommendation engine, we should not abdicate our authority nor relinquish our control to them. No matter how specific, valuable, or alluring the data—great leadership comes down to the human factor. Leaders must digest and assess AI inputs, but then chart their journeys using their insight, instinct, and humanity.

Acknowledgements

I would like to thank my family -- especially my wife -- for remaining incredibly supportive through all my hair-brained ideas ranging from writing and producing a horror movie, to going back to school in my mid-40s, to writing a book about finance automation. I could not have done any of that without you and am forever grateful.

I'd also like to thank the team at Leaders Press for turning this dream into a reality. Thank you for all your hard work, organization, and patience as we brought Deep Finance to life.

I am grateful for the brilliant professors and my incredible classmates in the Harvard Business Analytics Program (Go team #HBAP!). The vision and focus on digital transformation not only helped to clarify my own thinking on business intelligence but inspired this book.

Finally to all my business partners, leaders, mentors, co-workers, and teams from over the years. Thank you for helping me carve this path to finance automation. We did it the hard way! I hope through all our efforts we helped blaze a trail to automation for our brothers and sisters in arms in the fight against manual journal entries!

About the Author

A former Navy journalist, filmmaker, and business founder, Glenn Hopper has spent the past two decades helping startups transition to going concerns, operate at scale, and prepare for funding and/or acquisition. He is passionate about transforming the role of chief financial officer from historical reporter to forward-looking strategist. He has served as a finance leader in a variety of industries including telecommunications, retail, internet, and legal technology. He has a master's degree in finance with a graduate certificate in business analytics from Harvard University, and a master's degree in business administration from Regis University. Glenn is married with three children, two goldendoodles, and a neurotic cat. Glenn is also a member of American Mensa and volunteers his time for the Analytics Foundation, helping nonprofits to digitally transform their organizations. In his free time, Glenn is an avid runner and cyclist.